Mastery in Markets: Advanced Strategies for Seasoned Investors

Investing, Volume 3

Rey Regala

Published by Isaac Nangan, 2024.

MASTERY IN MARKETS: ADVANCED STRATEGIES FOR SEASONED INVESTORS

First edition. February 18, 2024.

ISBN: 979-8223114284

Written by Rey Regala.

Table of Contents

To Coleen, Sky and Neo. You are my inspirations.

Mastery in Markets: Advanced Strategies for Seasoned Investors

Rey Regala

Preface

Acknowledgments

First and foremost, I extend my deepest gratitude to the many mentors, colleagues, and industry leaders who have shared their invaluable insights and experiences with me over the years. Their wisdom has been instrumental in shaping the perspectives and strategies presented in this book.

Overview of the Investment Landscape for the Advanced Investor

The world of investing is perpetually evolving, marked by the emergence of new asset classes, the development of complex financial instruments, and an ever-changing global economic landscape. For the advanced investor, these changes present both unique challenges and unprecedented opportunities.

This book, "Mastery in Markets: Advanced Strategies for Seasoned Investors," is crafted to serve as a comprehensive guide for those who have already traversed the foundational aspects of investing and are looking to deepen their understanding and enhance their strategies in this dynamic arena.

The aim is not merely to provide a collection of advanced investment techniques and theories but to offer a holistic view of the contemporary investment landscape. This includes insights into the psychological aspects of investing, an understanding of the global macroeconomic environment, and a deep dive into complex instruments and strategies.

Each chapter in this book is structured to stand alone, allowing readers to focus on areas most relevant to their individual investment goals and strategies. While the book progresses logically, the seasoned investor will find value in each section, regardless of the order in which it is read.

Moreover, this book recognizes the importance of ethics and sustainability in modern investing. It discusses how these principles can be integrated into advanced investment strategies, not only to align with personal values but also to identify long-term, sustainable growth opportunities.

In writing this book, I have drawn upon my years of experience in the financial sector, coupled with extensive research and discussions with top investors and financial thinkers. The examples and case studies included are chosen to provide practical insights and to illustrate the application of the concepts discussed.

As the investment landscape continues to evolve, so too must the strategies and approaches of the investor. It is my hope that "Mastery in Markets" serves as a valuable resource in your continued journey in the complex and rewarding world of advanced investing.

Prologue

As we stand at the cusp of a new era in investing, it becomes increasingly clear that the traditional methods and strategies that once dominated the world of finance are no longer sufficient. The rapid advancement of technology, the globalization of markets, and the emergence of new and complex asset classes have transformed the landscape, necessitating a deeper, more nuanced understanding of investing.

This book, "Mastery in Markets: Advanced Strategies for Seasoned Investors," is born out of a recognition of this transformative era in the world of finance. It is a response to the growing need among advanced investors for a guide that goes beyond the basics, delving into the intricate and often nuanced strategies that define successful investing in today's world.

In this prologue, I want to set the stage for what you, as an advanced investor, can expect from this book. This is not a beginner's guide to investing; rather, it is a deep dive into the strategies, theories, and practices that are shaping the future of finance. It is a book that assumes a fundamental understanding of investment principles and builds upon that foundation to explore more sophisticated and advanced topics.

The focus of this book is on the application of these advanced strategies in real-world scenarios. Through a combination of theory, case studies, and practical examples, I aim to provide a comprehensive overview of the tools and techniques at the disposal of the seasoned investor. Whether it's navigating the complexities of alternative investments, understanding the intricacies of behavioral finance, or mastering the art of quantitative analysis, this book aims to equip you with the knowledge and insights needed to thrive in the modern financial landscape.

As we delve into these topics, I encourage you to approach this book not just as a source of information, but as a guide to thinking critically and creatively about investing. The world of finance is dynamic, and the most successful investors are those who are able to adapt, evolve, and think outside the box.

So, as you turn these pages, I invite you to embark on a journey of exploration and discovery. Let us delve into the advanced strategies that will define the next chapter of your investing journey, equipping you with the tools and insights needed to navigate the complexities of the modern financial world.

Chapter Overviews

Chapter 1: Advanced Portfolio Theory

This chapter delves into the complexities of portfolio construction and management for seasoned investors. It discusses integrating modern and post-modern portfolio theories, exploring advanced diversification strategies beyond traditional asset classes. The concept of risk parity and alternative risk premia are examined, using examples of how these approaches can optimize risk-adjusted returns.

Chapter 2: Quantitative Analysis and Algorithmic Trading

Here, the focus is on building predictive models for investing, highlighting both the techniques used and the potential pitfalls. The chapter covers the realm of high-frequency trading, discussing its opportunities and risks. It also examines the role of machine learning in investment decision-making, with practical examples of its application.

Chapter 3: Alternative Investments and Unconventional Assets

This chapter provides insights into investing in private equity, venture capital, real estate, infrastructure, commodities, cryptocurrencies, and blockchain technology. Each section not only explains the asset class but also provides real-world examples of successful and unsuccessful investments, highlighting best practices and common mistakes.

Chapter 4: Behavioral Finance and Investor Psychology

An exploration of how cognitive biases and emotional factors can impact investment decisions. This chapter emphasizes the importance of emotional discipline and offers strategies to counteract common biases. It also discusses contrarian investment strategies, providing case studies where going against the market consensus has yielded significant returns.

Chapter 5: Global Macro Strategies and Geopolitical Analysis

Focusing on the importance of understanding economic indicators and global political risks, this chapter discusses how these factors can impact markets. It also covers strategies for currency market investments, including detailed examples of successful forex trading strategies.

Chapter 6: Advanced Derivative Strategies

An in-depth look at options, futures, swaps, and structured products. This chapter explains how advanced investors use these instruments for hedging and speculation, with real-world examples of complex derivative strategies and their outcomes.

Chapter 7: Ethical Investing and Corporate Governance

This chapter discusses the principles of sustainable and responsible investing, the impact of corporate governance on investment returns, and how to integrate ESG (Environmental, Social, and Governance) criteria into investment analysis. It includes case studies demonstrating the long-term value of ethical investing.

Chapter 8: Tax Strategies and Efficient Asset Allocation

A guide to tax-optimized investment strategies, asset location, and the tax implications of various investment decisions. It also covers estate planning and wealth transfer techniques, providing practical examples of how these strategies can be implemented.

Chapter 9: Advanced Portfolio Management Techniques

This chapter focuses on dynamic asset allocation, tactical adjustments, stress testing, scenario analysis, and performance attribution. It provides advanced portfolio management tools and techniques, using real-life examples to illustrate their application.

Chapter 10: The Future of Investing

A forward-looking chapter that discusses emerging technologies, global economic trends, and how investors can adapt to a rapidly changing investment landscape. It also emphasizes the importance of continuous learning and adaptation for advanced investors.

Chapter 1: Advanced Portfolio Theory

1.1 Integrating Modern and Post-Modern Portfolio Theory

Modern Portfolio Theory (MPT), developed by Harry Markowitz in the 1950s, revolutionized the way we think about risk and return in finance. MPT's core principle is diversification, suggesting that an investor can achieve optimal portfolio construction by balancing assets that do not move in tandem. However, as financial markets have evolved, the limitations of MPT have become apparent, especially in its assumption of normally distributed returns and constant correlations.

Post-Modern Portfolio Theory (PMPT) emerged as a response to these limitations. PMPT focuses on the asymmetry of returns and investors' actual preferences concerning risk, emphasizing that investors are more concerned with downside risk than variance. This shift leads to strategies focusing on minimizing downside risk rather than simply balancing the mean and variance of portfolio returns.

Integrating MPT and PMPT involves recognizing the strengths and weaknesses of each approach. Investors should consider diversification (MPT) and be acutely aware of the asymmetry and extremes in returns (PMPT). This integration can be achieved by constructing portfolios that not only have a balanced risk-return profile but also are tailored to minimize significant losses during market downturns.

1.2 Advanced Diversification Strategies

Traditional diversification strategies often involve spreading investments across various asset classes like stocks, bonds, and cash. However, advanced diversification looks at additional dimensions, such as:

- **Factor Diversification:** Investing across different economic drivers or "factors" such as value, size, momentum, and quality. Each of these factors responds differently to economic conditions, offering a more nuanced approach to diversification.
- **Geographic Diversification:** Going beyond domestic markets to include international and emerging markets, recognizing that different economies may be at different stages of the economic cycle.
- **Asset-Class Diversification:** Incorporating non-traditional asset classes like real estate, commodities, private equity, and hedge funds, which often show different return characteristics compared to traditional stocks and bonds.

1.3 Risk Parity and Alternative Risk Premia

Risk Parity is a portfolio allocation strategy that focuses on allocating risk, rather than capital, equally among different asset classes. Unlike traditional portfolio strategies that allocate more capital to assets with higher expected returns (and hence, often higher risk), risk parity aims to balance the portfolio's risk contributions from each asset class. This approach often involves using leverage to increase the portfolio's exposure to lower-risk assets, such as bonds, to equalize their risk contribution with that of higher-risk assets like equities.

Alternative Risk Premia strategies seek to capture returns from sources other than traditional stock and bond markets. These include styles like carry (profiting from differentials in interest rates or yields), momentum (capitalizing on trends), and value (investing in assets that appear underpriced). By incorporating alternative risk premia into a portfolio, investors can potentially improve risk-adjusted returns and further diversify their investment strategies.

Both risk parity and alternative risk premia require a deep understanding of risk dynamics and the ability to implement sophisticated investment techniques. These strategies can offer advanced investors tools to navigate complex markets and achieve more consistent returns across different market environments.

1.1 Integrating Modern and Post-Modern Portfolio Theory

The integration of Modern Portfolio Theory (MPT) and Post-Modern Portfolio Theory (PMPT) represents a significant advancement in the field of portfolio management and investment strategy. This integration acknowledges that while the principles of MPT laid a solid foundation for portfolio diversification, the evolving financial markets demand a more nuanced approach, as offered by PMPT. Let's delve deeper into each theory and their integration.

Modern Portfolio Theory (MPT):

- **Foundation:** MPT, conceptualized by Harry Markowitz in the 1950s, revolutionized investment strategy with its emphasis on diversification. The core idea of MPT is that an investor can reduce portfolio risk and increase expected return by holding a diversified portfolio of assets, rather than individual securities.
- **Key Concepts:**
    - **Efficient Frontier:** MPT introduces the concept of the 'efficient frontier', a set of optimal portfolios offering the maximum possible expected return for a given level of risk.
    - **Correlation:** It stresses the importance of asset correlation, advocating for investment in assets that do not move in

tandem.

Post-Modern Portfolio Theory (PMPT):

- **Emergence:** As the financial landscape evolved, the limitations of MPT became evident, particularly its assumptions of normal distribution of returns and constant correlations. PMPT emerged to address these shortcomings.
- **Key Concepts:**
    - **Asymmetry of Returns:** PMPT places greater emphasis on the asymmetry of returns, recognizing that investors are more sensitive to losses than gains.
    - **Downside Risk:** It shifts the focus from balancing the mean and variance of portfolio returns to minimizing downside risk. This is in line with the real-world behavior of investors who are often more concerned about potential losses.

Integrating MPT and PMPT:

- **Holistic Approach:** The integration involves using the diversification principles of MPT while also incorporating the risk sensitivity and asymmetry considerations of PMPT.
- **Tailored Portfolio Construction:** Portfolios should be constructed not just to balance risk and return (as per MPT) but also to minimize potential large losses (as per PMPT). This might involve more sophisticated risk management strategies, such as tail risk hedging.
- **Dynamic Adjustment:** Given the evolving nature of market conditions and correlations, this integrated approach also calls for dynamic portfolio adjustment.

Unlike the static view of MPT, it involves regularly reassessing and rebalancing the portfolio in response to changing market dynamics and investor objectives.

Practical Example: Consider an investor using MPT principles to diversify across stocks, bonds, and commodities. To integrate PMPT, the investor might further refine the portfolio by adding investments that specifically target downside protection, such as options or assets that tend to perform well during market downturns (like certain types of bonds or defensive stocks). The investor would also monitor and adjust the portfolio more actively, taking into account changing market conditions and asymmetries in asset returns.

In conclusion, integrating MPT and PMPT allows investors to benefit from the diversification and risk management principles of both theories, resulting in portfolios that are not only diversified but also more aligned with the investor's risk tolerance and market realities. This approach is particularly relevant in today's complex and rapidly changing financial markets.

Modern Portfolio Theory (MPT):

Modern Portfolio Theory (MPT), as conceptualized by Harry Markowitz in the 1950s, indeed represents a pivotal moment in the evolution of investment strategy. Its principles have fundamentally shaped how investors approach portfolio construction, emphasizing the role of diversification in achieving a desirable balance between risk and return. Here's a more detailed look at the foundational elements and key concepts of MPT:

Foundation of Modern Portfolio Theory (MPT)

- **Origins:** MPT emerged as a groundbreaking approach in the 1950s, shifting the focus from individual asset selection to the composition of the entire portfolio.
- **Central Premise:** The theory posits that by diversifying across a range of assets, investors can reduce the overall risk of their portfolio while maintaining, or even enhancing, the expected return. This diversification benefit stems from the combination of assets that are not perfectly correlated.

Key Concepts of Modern Portfolio Theory

Efficient Frontier

- **Definition:** The Efficient Frontier is a central concept in MPT, representing a set of portfolios that offer the highest expected return for a given level of risk, or the lowest risk for a given level of expected return.
- **Visualization:** Graphically, the Efficient Frontier is depicted in a risk-return space, with risk (usually measured as standard deviation) on the x-axis and expected return on the y-axis.
- **Optimal Portfolios:** Portfolios that lie on the Efficient Frontier are considered optimal because any other

portfolio with the same level of risk will have a lower expected return, and any portfolio with the same expected return will have a higher level of risk.

Correlation

- **Role of Correlation:** MPT underscores the importance of the correlation between assets in a portfolio. Correlation measures how assets move in relation to each other.
- **Diversification Benefits:** Assets with low or negative correlations provide greater diversification benefits. The idea is that when some assets are declining in value, others may be increasing or not falling as much, thus reducing the overall volatility of the portfolio.
- **Strategic Asset Allocation:** Strategic asset allocation involves selecting a mix of asset classes (like stocks, bonds, real estate) with varying correlations to construct a portfolio that aligns with an investor's risk tolerance and investment objectives.

By advocating for the construction of diversified portfolios based on these principles, MPT laid the groundwork for much of the portfolio management techniques used today. It provided a systematic, quantitative approach to portfolio diversification, moving away from the earlier, more anecdotal methods of investing.

The enduring relevance of MPT lies in its simplicity and the intuitive appeal of its core premise: diversification not only reduces risk but can do so without necessarily compromising returns. As financial markets have grown more complex, the principles of MPT continue to influence investment strategies, though they are now often blended with more contemporary theories and methods to address the evolving nature of financial markets.

Post-Modern Portfolio Theory (PMPT):

Post-Modern Portfolio Theory (PMPT) emerged as a response to the evolving complexities of the financial markets and the recognized limitations of Modern Portfolio Theory (MPT). PMPT adapts and extends the principles of MPT to better align with the realities of investor behavior and the nature of financial returns. Let's explore the emergence and key concepts of PMPT in more detail:

Emergence of Post-Modern Portfolio Theory

- **Context:** While MPT marked a significant advance in investment strategy, over time, its assumptions – particularly regarding the normal distribution of returns and constant correlations – were observed to be overly simplistic for the dynamic nature of financial markets.
- **Response to Limitations:** PMPT emerged as a more flexible and realistic framework, taking into account the deviations from the assumptions of MPT. It was developed to address the complexities and irregularities that are often observed in real-world financial markets.

Key Concepts of Post-Modern Portfolio Theory

Asymmetry of Returns

- **Definition:** PMPT places a strong emphasis on the asymmetry of returns, acknowledging that the distribution of investment returns is not always symmetrical or normal. This means that investment returns can exhibit skewed patterns, with periods of extreme gains or losses.
- **Investor Sensitivity:** The theory recognizes that investors react differently to gains and losses, often exhibiting more sensitivity to losses. This phenomenon is also supported by behavioral finance studies, which show that the pain of

losing is psychologically about twice as powerful as the pleasure of gaining (a concept known as loss aversion).

- **Implication for Portfolio Management:** Understanding the asymmetry of returns leads to a more nuanced approach to portfolio construction, where the focus is on managing the risks associated with extreme market movements, particularly on the downside.

Downside Risk

- **Shift in Focus:** PMPT shifts the focus from the traditional mean-variance optimization (central to MPT) to a concentration on minimizing downside risk. Downside risk is the potential for loss in the value of an investment.
- **Real-World Alignment:** This shift is more aligned with how investors actually perceive and react to risk. Many investors are more concerned about the potential for significant losses (downside risk) than the overall volatility (variance) of their portfolio.
- **Risk Management Techniques:** To manage downside risk, PMPT advocates for techniques such as stress testing, scenario analysis, and the use of financial instruments that can provide protection in declining markets, such as put options or assets with inverse correlations to traditional markets.

By incorporating these concepts, PMPT offers a more comprehensive and realistic approach to portfolio management, especially in turbulent or atypical market conditions. It acknowledges that market returns often do not follow a normal distribution and that investors have asymmetric preferences regarding gains and losses. This theory guides investors in creating portfolios that are not only diversified but also structured to minimize the impact of severe market downturns, aligning more closely with investor behavior and the realities of market dynamics.

Integrating MPT and PMPT:

The integration of Modern Portfolio Theory (MPT) and Post-Modern Portfolio Theory (PMPT) represents a comprehensive approach to portfolio management that combines the strengths of both theories. This integrated approach is particularly relevant in today's complex financial environment, where market conditions and investor needs are constantly evolving. Let's delve into the key aspects of this integration:

Holistic Approach

- **Combining Principles:** The integration involves utilizing the diversification principles of MPT along with the considerations of risk sensitivity and return asymmetry from PMPT. This means acknowledging the benefits of diversification across different asset classes (as per MPT) while also being mindful of the non-normal distribution of returns and the asymmetrical reaction of investors to gains and losses (as highlighted in PMPT).
- **Balanced Focus:** This approach ensures that portfolio construction is not solely fixated on the mean and variance of returns (as in MPT) but also on the realities of how returns are actually distributed and how investors perceive risk (as recognized in PMPT).

Tailored Portfolio Construction

- **Customization:** Portfolios are constructed to balance risk and return (as per MPT), but with a stronger emphasis on minimizing potential large losses (as per PMPT). This approach acknowledges that minimizing downside risk can be more aligned with investor preferences.
- **Sophisticated Risk Management:** This might involve

employing advanced risk management strategies such as tail risk hedging, which focuses on protecting against rare but severe market events. Such strategies could include the use of derivatives, alternative investments, or dynamic asset allocation techniques that adjust to market volatility.

Dynamic Adjustment

- **Adaptability:** Recognizing the dynamic nature of market conditions and correlations, this integrated approach emphasizes the need for continual portfolio reassessment and rebalancing. Unlike the more static perspective of MPT, it acknowledges that market conditions, investor goals, and risk profiles are not static and must be regularly reviewed and adjusted.
- **Responsive Strategy:** Dynamic adjustment involves being responsive to both short-term market fluctuations and long-term economic changes. This might include tactical asset allocation shifts in response to market cycles, adjusting the portfolio in anticipation of economic trends, or rebalancing to maintain alignment with an investor's changing risk tolerance or life circumstances.

In summary, integrating MPT and PMPT into a cohesive investment strategy offers a more nuanced and adaptable approach to portfolio management. It combines the traditional wisdom of diversification with a deeper understanding of risk dynamics and investor behavior. This holistic method is particularly suitable for navigating the increasingly complex and unpredictable financial markets of today, aiming not just for optimal returns but also for resilience against downside risks.

1.2 Advanced Diversification Strategies

Advanced diversification strategies involve a more sophisticated approach to constructing an investment portfolio, going beyond the traditional mix of stocks, bonds, and cash. These strategies recognize that a multi-dimensional approach to diversification can better manage risk and enhance returns. Let's explore these advanced strategies in detail:

Factor Diversification

- **Concept:** Factor diversification is based on investing across different economic drivers or 'factors' that influence asset returns. Common factors include value (stocks priced low relative to their fundamental value), size (small-cap vs. large-cap), momentum (trending assets), and quality (companies with stable earnings and low debt).
- **Application:** Investors can implement factor diversification by selecting assets or funds that target these specific factors. For instance, a momentum-focused fund might invest in stocks exhibiting an upward price trend. The key is to combine factors that are less correlated with each other, as this can reduce overall portfolio volatility.
- **Benefits:** This approach can provide a more granular level of diversification, potentially leading to better risk-adjusted returns, as different factors may outperform under different market conditions.

Geographic Diversification

- **Concept:** Geographic diversification involves spreading investments across various global markets. This strategy capitalizes on the fact that different economies and markets can be at different stages of the growth cycle, and they respond differently to regional and global economic events.
- **Application:** An investor might allocate a portion of their portfolio to international developed markets, emerging markets, or specific countries or regions. This can be done through international mutual funds, ETFs, or direct investments in foreign stocks.
- **Benefits:** Geographic diversification can reduce the risk of concentrating investments in any single country or region. It can also tap into growth opportunities in different parts of the world, especially in emerging markets, which might have higher growth potential compared to developed markets.

Asset-Class Diversification

- **Concept:** Asset-class diversification involves including a variety of asset classes in a portfolio, beyond the traditional mix. This includes real estate, commodities, private equity, hedge funds, and even digital assets like cryptocurrencies.
- **Application:** Investors can gain exposure to these asset classes through various vehicles such as REITs (for real estate), commodity futures or ETFs, private equity funds, and hedge funds. Each of these asset classes has its own risk and return profile and behaves differently in various economic conditions.

- **Benefits:** By diversifying into non-traditional asset classes, investors can potentially reduce overall portfolio risk and improve returns. For example, commodities often have a low correlation with stocks and can act as a hedge against inflation. Similarly, private equity can offer higher return potential, albeit with higher risk and lower liquidity.

Integrating Advanced Diversification

Integrating these advanced diversification strategies involves carefully balancing the portfolio across different factors, geographies, and asset classes. It requires a thorough understanding of the correlations between these dimensions and their individual risk profiles. This process often involves continuous monitoring and rebalancing to ensure the portfolio remains aligned with the investor's goals and market conditions.

In summary, advanced diversification strategies offer a more robust approach to portfolio construction. By considering factors, geographic regions, and a broader range of asset classes, investors can create a well-rounded portfolio that is better equipped to navigate the complexities of today's financial markets.

Factor Diversification

Factor diversification is an advanced approach to portfolio construction that goes beyond the traditional asset class diversification. It focuses on different economic drivers or 'factors' that have been found to explain differences in returns between securities. Here's a detailed look at the concept, application, and benefits of factor diversification:

Concept of Factor Diversification

- **Defining Factors:** Factors are specific characteristics or attributes that can explain differences in return across various securities. They are essentially the underlying drivers of asset returns.
- **Common Factors:**
    - **Value:** Investing in stocks that are priced low relative to their fundamental value. Value stocks are typically those that are undervalued by the market but have strong potential for growth.
    - **Size:** Involves focusing on the market capitalization of companies. Small-cap stocks (i.e., companies with smaller market capitalization) might behave differently than large-cap stocks.
    - **Momentum:** This factor involves investing in assets that are currently exhibiting an upward price trend. The momentum strategy bets on the continuation of existing market trends.
    - **Quality:** Quality investing targets companies with stable earnings, low debt, and strong balance sheets. These companies are often considered more resilient and less risky.

Application of Factor Diversification

- **Selection of Assets or Funds:** Factor diversification is implemented by selecting assets or funds that specifically target these factors. For instance, a value-focused fund would concentrate on undervalued stocks, while a momentum fund would invest in fast-moving trends in the market.

- **Combining Factors:** The key to effective factor diversification is combining factors that are less correlated with each other. This helps in reducing overall portfolio volatility. For example, a portfolio could include a mix of value and momentum stocks, as these factors often perform well in different market environments.

Benefits of Factor Diversification

- **Enhanced Diversification:** Factor diversification offers a more granular approach to diversifying a portfolio. By investing across different factors, an investor can potentially reduce risk more effectively than by only diversifying across traditional asset classes.
- **Improved Risk-Adjusted Returns:** Different factors may outperform under various market conditions. By diversifying across multiple factors, a portfolio can potentially achieve better risk-adjusted returns. For instance, value stocks may perform well in some market phases, while momentum or quality stocks may excel in others.
- **Adaptability to Market Conditions:** Factor investing allows portfolios to be more adaptable to changing market conditions. Investors can overweight or underweight certain factors based on market forecasts or economic outlooks, potentially enhancing returns or reducing risk in

different phases of the market cycle.

In summary, factor diversification represents a sophisticated and nuanced approach to portfolio construction, enabling investors to tap into specific drivers of returns. This strategy can offer benefits in terms of enhanced diversification and potentially improved risk-adjusted returns, especially in a complex and ever-changing market environment.

Geographic Diversification

Geographic diversification is a key strategy in portfolio management that entails spreading investments across various global markets to reduce risk and capitalize on different growth opportunities. This strategy is rooted in the recognition that different economies and markets operate in distinct cycles and respond differently to economic events. Here's an in-depth look at the concept, application, and benefits of geographic diversification:

Concept of Geographic Diversification

- **Diversifying Across Markets:** Geographic diversification is based on the premise that by investing in a variety of countries or regions, an investor can reduce the risks associated with any single geographic area. This is particularly important because different markets and economies can exhibit varying levels of growth, stability, and risk.
- **Growth Cycle Variations:** Different economies and markets can be at different stages of the growth cycle at any given time. For example, emerging markets might be experiencing rapid growth while some developed markets might be in a more mature stage. These differences can lead to varied investment opportunities and risks.

Application of Geographic Diversification

- **Portfolio Allocation:** Investors can apply geographic diversification by allocating a portion of their portfolio to international developed markets, emerging markets, or specific countries or regions. The exact allocation depends on the investor's risk tolerance, investment goals, and market outlook.

- **Investment Vehicles:** Geographic diversification can be achieved through various investment vehicles, such as:
    - **International Mutual Funds:** These funds invest in a diverse range of stocks across different countries and regions.
    - **Exchange-Traded Funds (ETFs):** ETFs offer an easy and efficient way to gain exposure to international markets. There are ETFs that focus on specific regions, countries, or global indexes.
    - **Direct Investments:** Investors can also choose to directly invest in foreign stocks, though this requires more knowledge of the individual markets and entails additional risks and considerations, such as currency risk.

Benefits of Geographic Diversification

- **Risk Reduction:** By diversifying geographically, investors can reduce the risk associated with concentrating their investments in one country or region. This is especially relevant in the face of country-specific risks such as political instability, economic downturns, or regulatory changes.
- **Access to Global Opportunities:** Geographic diversification allows investors to tap into growth opportunities in different parts of the world. For instance, emerging markets may offer higher growth potential and unique investment opportunities compared to more developed markets.
- **Balanced Portfolio Performance:** Different markets may perform differently in response to global economic events. Geographic diversification can help in balancing the overall performance of a portfolio, as gains in one region

may offset losses in another.

In conclusion, geographic diversification is a critical component of a well-rounded investment strategy. By allocating assets across various global markets, investors can mitigate country-specific risks, capitalize on different economic growth phases, and potentially achieve a more stable and balanced portfolio performance. This strategy is particularly significant in a globalized economy where regional events can have widespread impacts on financial markets.

Asset-Class Diversification

Asset-class diversification is a strategic approach in portfolio management that involves expanding the range of asset classes within a portfolio beyond traditional investments. This strategy recognizes the unique characteristics and benefits of various asset classes, including their differing responses to economic conditions. Let's explore the concept, application, and benefits of asset-class diversification:

Concept of Asset-Class Diversification

- **Broadening the Investment Spectrum:** Asset-class diversification is about including a wide range of asset classes in a portfolio. While traditional portfolios focus on stocks, bonds, and cash, this approach incorporates additional asset classes.
- **Non-Traditional Asset Classes:** These include real estate, commodities, private equity, hedge funds, and digital assets like cryptocurrencies. Each of these asset classes has distinct risk and return profiles and reacts differently to market conditions and economic cycles.

Application of Asset-Class Diversification

- **Investment Vehicles for Diversification:**
    - **Real Estate Investment Trusts (REITs):** REITs offer a way to invest in real estate without having to buy or manage property directly. They are known for providing dividend income along with capital appreciation potential.
    - **Commodity Futures or ETFs:** These instruments allow investors to gain exposure to commodities like oil, gold, and agricultural products. Commodities can be a good hedge against inflation and have a low correlation with stock

markets.
    - **Private Equity Funds:** These funds invest in private companies and can offer higher returns, albeit with higher risk and lower liquidity compared to public markets.
    - **Hedge Funds:** Hedge funds employ a variety of strategies to earn active return, or alpha, for their investors. They might use leverage, derivatives, and short selling to achieve their investment objectives.
    - **Cryptocurrencies and Digital Assets:** These represent a newer asset class and offer exposure to the digital currency market, which is characterized by high volatility and potential for significant returns.

Benefits of Asset-Class Diversification

- **Risk Reduction:** By diversifying into different asset classes, investors can reduce the overall risk of their portfolio. This is because these asset classes often have low correlations with one another; when one class is underperforming, another may be outperforming, thus balancing the overall portfolio performance.
- **Inflation Hedging:** Certain asset classes like commodities and real estate are known to act as hedges against inflation. Their values often increase when inflation rises, thereby protecting the purchasing power of the investment portfolio.
- **Potential for Improved Returns:** Diversifying into non-traditional asset classes can improve the return potential of a portfolio. For example, private equity may offer higher growth potential, and commodities can provide returns that are independent of stock and bond market movements.

- **Access to Unique Opportunities:** Asset-class diversification allows investors to tap into unique investment opportunities and trends that are not available in traditional asset classes. This could include investing in emerging technologies through venture capital or participating in the growth of new markets through cryptocurrencies.

In conclusion, asset-class diversification is a sophisticated strategy that can enhance a portfolio's resilience, offer new avenues for growth, and potentially improve the overall risk-return profile. By incorporating a variety of asset classes, investors can achieve a more robust and well-rounded investment portfolio capable of navigating various market environments.

Integrating Advanced Diversification

Integrating advanced diversification strategies into a portfolio is a nuanced and dynamic process. It involves a comprehensive approach to portfolio construction that considers various dimensions of diversification, including factors, geographies, and a broad spectrum of asset classes. Let's delve into how this integration can be effectively achieved:

Understanding Correlations and Risk Profiles

- **Analyzing Correlations:** A crucial step in advanced diversification is understanding how different investments correlate with each other. The goal is to combine assets in a way that reduces overall portfolio volatility. For instance, during a market downturn, certain asset classes like treasuries may perform differently than stocks, providing a cushion against losses.
- **Risk Profile Assessment:** Each investment type carries its own risk profile. For example, commodities may offer inflation protection but can be highly volatile, while real estate may provide steady income but can be illiquid. Understanding these characteristics is essential to creating a balanced portfolio.

Strategic Portfolio Construction

- **Combining Diversification Strategies:** The portfolio should be constructed by blending different types of diversification:
    - **Factor Diversification:** Including a mix of value, size, momentum, and quality investments.
    - **Geographic Diversification:** Spreading investments across various global markets.

    - **Asset-Class Diversification:** Incorporating traditional and non-traditional assets like stocks, bonds, real estate, commodities, private equity, hedge funds, and digital assets.
- **Alignment with Investor Goals:** The diversified portfolio must align with the investor's financial goals, risk tolerance, and investment horizon. For instance, a retirement portfolio might prioritize income and stability, while a growth-oriented investor might focus more on equities and private equity.

Continuous Monitoring and Rebalancing

- **Market Dynamics:** Financial markets are dynamic, and asset correlations can change over time. Continuous monitoring helps in identifying these shifts and understanding their impact on the portfolio.
- **Rebalancing Strategy:** Regular rebalancing is necessary to maintain the intended asset allocation. This may involve selling assets that have grown to represent too large a portion of the portfolio and buying more of those that have underperformed, thus maintaining the desired risk level.
- **Adaptation to Changes:** The integration of advanced diversification strategies also involves adapting the portfolio in response to significant economic, geopolitical, or market changes. This proactive approach can help in capitalizing on emerging opportunities or mitigating risks.

Utilizing Technology and Expertise

- **Analytical Tools:** Leveraging advanced analytical tools and software can aid in understanding the complex interactions between different portfolio components. These tools can provide insights into risk exposure, return potential, and correlation dynamics.

- **Professional Guidance:** Given the complexity involved in integrating advanced diversification strategies, seeking advice from financial advisors or investment professionals can be beneficial. They can provide expertise in portfolio construction, risk management, and ongoing portfolio oversight.

In summary, integrating advanced diversification strategies is not a set-and-forget process but a continuous journey of adaptation and refinement. It involves a deep understanding of various investment dimensions, a strategic approach to combining them, and an ongoing commitment to monitoring and adjusting the portfolio as needed. This comprehensive approach can help investors build a resilient and well-optimized portfolio suited to their unique objectives and the ever-changing market landscape.

1.3 Risk Parity and Alternative Risk Premia

The concepts of Risk Parity and Alternative Risk Premia represent sophisticated approaches to portfolio management, focusing on risk allocation and tapping into diverse sources of returns. Let's explore these strategies in more detail:

Risk Parity

Concept

- **Risk Allocation Focus:** Risk Parity is a portfolio allocation strategy that emphasizes equalizing risk contributions from different asset classes, rather than allocating capital based solely on expected returns.
- **Balancing Risk Contributions:** The strategy aims to ensure that no single asset class disproportionately contributes to the overall risk of the portfolio. This is a departure from traditional allocation strategies where higher capital is often allocated to higher-return (and higher-risk) assets.

Application

- **Using Leverage:** Risk Parity often involves the use of leverage to enhance the portfolio's exposure to lower-risk assets. For example, to balance the risk contribution of bonds with that of equities, leverage may be applied to the bond component of the portfolio.

- **Diverse Asset Classes:** The strategy typically involves a mix of diverse asset classes, including equities, bonds, commodities, and possibly alternative investments, each with different risk profiles.

Benefits

- **Risk Diversification:** By balancing risk across various asset classes, risk parity aims to achieve more stable and consistent portfolio performance, particularly in volatile markets.
- **Potential for Improved Risk-Adjusted Returns:** The strategy seeks to optimize the risk-return trade-off of the portfolio, potentially leading to better risk-adjusted returns over the long term.

Alternative Risk Premia
Concept

- **Beyond Traditional Markets:** Alternative Risk Premia strategies focus on capturing returns from sources beyond the traditional equity and bond markets. These strategies identify and exploit various risk premia (risk-related returns) that are not typically accessed in conventional investing.

Styles

- **Carry:** This style involves profiting from the differential in interest rates or yields across different markets or instruments. For example, in the currency market, an investor might borrow in a low-interest-rate currency and invest in a higher-yielding currency.

- **Momentum:** This strategy capitalizes on the continuation of existing market trends. For instance, buying assets that have been performing well recently, with the expectation that the trend will continue.
- **Value:** Value investing focuses on assets that appear underpriced relative to their fundamental value. It's based on the belief that the market will eventually recognize and correct the undervaluation.

Application

- **Diversified Strategies:** Investors can incorporate alternative risk premia strategies into their portfolios through various financial instruments, including derivatives, ETFs, and mutual funds that are structured to target these specific premia.

Benefits

- **Enhanced Diversification:** These strategies offer additional layers of diversification, as they are based on risk factors that are often different from those driving traditional stock and bond markets.
- **Potential for Non-Correlated Returns:** Alternative risk premia can provide returns that are less correlated with the broader market, potentially reducing overall portfolio volatility and enhancing risk-adjusted returns.

Integrating Risk Parity and Alternative Risk Premia

- **Complementary Strategies:** Both risk parity and alternative risk premia can be integrated into a broader portfolio to enhance diversification and risk management. While risk parity focuses on balancing risk across traditional asset classes, alternative risk premia provide access to different sources of returns.

- **Holistic Portfolio Construction:** By combining these strategies, investors can construct a more resilient portfolio that is not overly dependent on the performance of any single asset class or traditional market factor. This integration can lead to a more robust investment approach, especially in complex and unpredictable market environments.

In conclusion, Risk Parity and Alternative Risk Premia are advanced investment strategies that offer sophisticated ways to manage risk and seek returns. Their integration into a portfolio can lead to enhanced diversification, potentially improved risk-adjusted returns, and a more nuanced approach to navigating the financial markets.

Risk Parity

Risk Parity is a sophisticated portfolio allocation strategy that redefines the traditional approach to building an investment portfolio. Instead of focusing primarily on capital allocation based on expected returns, Risk Parity emphasizes the equalization of risk contributions from various asset classes. Let's explore this concept, its application, and the benefits it offers:

Concept

- **Risk Allocation Focus:** The central idea of Risk Parity is to allocate investment risk, rather than capital, equally among different asset classes. It's a strategy that seeks a more balanced risk distribution within a portfolio.
- **Balancing Risk Contributions:** Traditional portfolio strategies often allocate more capital to assets with higher expected returns, which usually carry higher risk (like stocks). Risk Parity, by contrast, aims to balance the risk each asset class contributes to the portfolio. This balance is intended to reduce the dominance of any single asset class in determining the portfolio's overall risk profile.

Application

- **Using Leverage:** A key aspect of Risk Parity is the use of leverage to adjust the risk contribution of different asset classes. For instance, in a traditional portfolio, equities often have a higher risk profile compared to bonds. To balance this, leverage can be applied to bonds, increasing their risk profile to a level more comparable to equities.
- **Diverse Asset Classes:** Risk Parity involves diversifying across a variety of asset classes. This isn't limited to just stocks and bonds but can also include commodities, real

estate, and potentially alternative investments. The goal is to include a mix of assets that respond differently to various market conditions, thereby diversifying risk.

Benefits

- **Risk Diversification:** One of the primary advantages of Risk Parity is improved risk diversification. By ensuring that no single asset class disproportionately affects the portfolio's risk, the strategy aims to provide more stable and consistent performance across different market environments.
- **Potential for Improved Risk-Adjusted Returns:** Through balanced risk contribution, Risk Parity seeks to optimize the risk-return trade-off. This could potentially lead to better risk-adjusted returns over the long term, as the strategy aims to capture returns from a broader set of market conditions and asset classes, rather than relying heavily on the performance of high-risk assets.

Conclusion

Risk Parity represents a shift from traditional capital allocation methods, focusing instead on an equal distribution of risk across various asset classes. Its use of leverage to balance risk contributions and its incorporation of diverse asset classes make it a unique and potentially effective strategy, especially for investors seeking stable, long-term performance with a keen eye on risk management. By applying the principles of Risk Parity, investors can aim for a portfolio that navigates through different market cycles with a more consistent risk profile.

Alternative Risk Premia

Alternative Risk Premia strategies represent a more nuanced approach to investment, seeking returns from sources that are typically not accessed in conventional stock and bond market investing. These strategies are designed to exploit different risk premia, providing investors with unique opportunities for portfolio diversification and enhanced returns. Let's delve deeper into the concept, styles, application, and benefits of Alternative Risk Premia:

Concept

- **Beyond Traditional Markets:** The core idea of Alternative Risk Premia strategies is to capture returns from risk factors beyond the traditional equity and bond markets. These strategies look for alternative sources of return that arise from risk premia, which are the rewards investors receive for taking on certain types of risk.
- **Exploiting Risk Premia:** Unlike traditional investing, which often focuses on capital growth through stock appreciation or income via bonds, Alternative Risk Premia strategies focus on different, often less explored, sources of risk and return.

Styles

- **Carry:** The carry strategy involves profiting from the differential in interest rates or yields. In the currency market, for instance, this might mean borrowing in a low-interest-rate currency and investing in a higher-yielding currency. Carry trades can also be applied in bond markets and commodities.
- **Momentum:** This strategy capitalizes on the continuation of existing market trends. It involves buying assets that have been performing well over a recent period, under the

premise that these trends are likely to continue in the short to medium term.

- **Value:** Value investing is about finding assets that appear underpriced relative to their fundamental value. This strategy relies on the belief that the market will eventually recognize and correct this undervaluation, leading to potential profit for investors who identified and invested in these undervalued assets early.

Application

- **Diversified Strategies:** Investors can apply Alternative Risk Premia strategies through a variety of financial instruments. This includes derivatives, exchange-traded funds (ETFs), and mutual funds specifically designed to target these risk premia.
- **Structural Integration:** These strategies can be integrated into a broader portfolio to enhance diversification and target specific risk-return objectives. They can be tailored to suit different investment horizons, risk tolerances, and market outlooks.

Benefits

- **Enhanced Diversification:** Alternative Risk Premia strategies provide additional layers of diversification for a portfolio. They are based on risk factors that often behave differently from the traditional equity and bond markets, thereby broadening the diversification base.
- **Potential for Non-Correlated Returns:** One of the key benefits of these strategies is the potential for returns that are less correlated with broader market movements. This

can be particularly valuable during periods of market stress or downturns in traditional markets.

- **Improved Risk-Adjusted Returns:** By tapping into diverse sources of return, Alternative Risk Premia strategies can enhance the overall risk-adjusted performance of a portfolio. They offer avenues to potentially improve returns while managing risk exposure.

Conclusion

Alternative Risk Premia strategies offer investors a sophisticated way to diversify their portfolios and access potential sources of return that are not solely tied to the performance of the stock or bond markets. By exploiting various risk premia, these strategies can provide a more diversified investment approach, potentially leading to improved risk-adjusted returns and a more resilient portfolio in varying market conditions.

Integrating Risk Parity and Alternative Risk Premia

Integrating Risk Parity and Alternative Risk Premia strategies can create a robust framework for portfolio construction, providing a comprehensive approach to diversification and risk management. This integration leverages the strengths of both strategies to build a portfolio that is resilient, adaptable, and potentially more efficient in terms of risk-adjusted returns. Let's explore how these strategies can be complementary and how they contribute to holistic portfolio construction:

Complementary Strategies

- **Balanced Risk with Diverse Returns:** Risk Parity's focus on balancing risk contributions from different asset classes complements the Alternative Risk Premia approach of tapping into varied sources of returns. While Risk Parity ensures that the portfolio is not overly dependent on any single asset class for its risk profile, Alternative Risk Premia seek returns based on different market factors and risk exposures.
- **Broadened Diversification:** By integrating these two strategies, a portfolio can achieve a broader level of diversification. Risk Parity enhances diversification across traditional asset classes, and Alternative Risk Premia extend this diversification into areas not typically covered by conventional stock and bond investments.

Holistic Portfolio Construction

- **Resilience in Diverse Market Conditions:** Combining Risk Parity and Alternative Risk Premia can lead to a portfolio that is more resilient across various market conditions. Risk Parity aims to stabilize the portfolio's performance across different economic cycles, while Alternative Risk Premia can provide non-correlated returns that may cushion the portfolio in times of market stress.

- **Customization to Investor Needs:** This integrated approach allows for a more tailored portfolio construction that aligns with specific investor goals and risk tolerances. By leveraging both strategies, investors can fine-tune their portfolios to target desired risk-return profiles.
- **Adaptability:** The combined approach is highly adaptable. It allows for dynamic adjustments based on evolving market conditions, ensuring that the portfolio remains aligned with the investor's objectives. This adaptability is crucial in navigating complex and unpredictable market environments.

Implementation Considerations

- **Risk Management:** Effective risk management is key when integrating these strategies. Investors need to be mindful of the risks associated with leverage in Risk Parity and the specific risks inherent in the various Alternative Risk Premia strategies.
- **Continuous Monitoring and Rebalancing:** This integrated portfolio requires ongoing monitoring and periodic rebalancing to maintain the desired risk balance and to adapt to changes in market conditions.
- **Expertise and Analysis:** Implementing and managing a portfolio that combines Risk Parity with Alternative Risk Premia may require a higher level of expertise and analytical capabilities. Investors might consider consulting

with financial advisors or using sophisticated investment tools for effective implementation.

Conclusion

Integrating Risk Parity and Alternative Risk Premia strategies can offer a powerful combination for modern portfolio construction. This approach provides a comprehensive framework for diversification, balancing traditional asset classes while exploiting alternative sources of returns. It can lead to a more nuanced and potentially more effective investment strategy, particularly suited for investors looking to navigate the complexities of today's financial markets with a robust and flexible portfolio.

Chapter 2: Quantitative Analysis and Algorithmic Trading

2.1 Building Predictive Models: Techniques and Pitfalls

Techniques:

- **Statistical Analysis and Econometrics:** Utilizing statistical methods to analyze historical data and identify potential trends and patterns.
- **Machine Learning Algorithms:** Employing advanced algorithms that can learn from data and make predictions or decisions based on that learning.
- **Time Series Analysis:** Specialized techniques for analyzing time-ordered data points, often crucial in financial markets where data points are collected over time.

Pitfalls:

- **Overfitting:** Creating models that are too complex and fit the nuances of historical data too closely, resulting in poor performance in unseen data.
- **Data Quality Issues:** The reliability of the models is heavily dependent on the quality of the input data. Inaccurate or incomplete data can lead to misleading results.

- **Ignoring Market Regime Changes:** Models that fail to account for changes in market regimes or structural breaks can become obsolete or ineffective.

2.2 High-Frequency Trading: Opportunities and Risks
Opportunities:

- **Arbitrage Opportunities:** Exploiting price discrepancies across different markets or securities in fractions of a second.
- **Market Making:** Providing liquidity to markets by constantly buying and selling securities, earning small profits on the bid-ask spread.
- **Speed:** The ability to execute trades much faster than human traders, capitalizing on opportunities that exist for only a short period.

Risks:

- **Market Impact and Instability:** High-frequency trading can contribute to increased volatility and sudden market swings.
- **Systemic Risks:** The interconnectedness of markets means that errors or anomalies in high-frequency trading systems can have widespread effects.
- **Regulatory and Ethical Considerations:** High-frequency trading faces scrutiny regarding its impact on market fairness and integrity.

2.3 Machine Learning in Investment Decision Making
Application:

- **Pattern Recognition:** Identifying complex patterns in market data that might be indicative of future price movements.
- **Predictive Analytics:** Using historical data to predict future market trends or asset price movements.
- **Sentiment Analysis:** Analyzing news, social media, and financial reports to gauge market sentiment.

Challenges and Considerations:

- **Interpretability:** Many machine learning models, especially deep learning models, are often considered 'black boxes' with limited interpretability.
- **Data Overfitting:** Similar to predictive models, machine learning algorithms are susceptible to overfitting if not properly validated.
- **Dynamic Markets:** Financial markets are constantly changing, and algorithms need regular updates and adjustments to remain relevant.

This chapter of "Quantitative Analysis and Algorithmic Trading" provides an in-depth look at the sophisticated techniques used in modern investing, along with their associated opportunities and challenges. It aims to equip advanced investors with the knowledge to navigate this complex yet increasingly important aspect of the investment world.

2.1 Building Predictive Models: Techniques and Pitfalls

In the realm of investment, predictive modeling has become a cornerstone for decision-making. Advanced investors leverage various techniques to forecast market movements and asset prices. However, the efficacy of these models depends on both the methodology employed and awareness of potential pitfalls.

Techniques

- **Statistical Analysis and Econometrics:**
  - This involves applying statistical methods to historical financial data to uncover trends and patterns. Techniques like regression analysis, hypothesis testing, and variance analysis are common.
  - Econometrics integrates economic theory with statistical methods, providing a more robust framework for analyzing economic data and forecasting financial trends.
- **Machine Learning Algorithms:**
  - Advanced algorithms that learn from historical data can be extremely powerful in predicting future market movements. These include supervised learning models like regression and classification, and unsupervised learning models

    like clustering.
  - Deep learning, a subset of machine learning involving neural networks, is increasingly being used for more complex financial forecasting.
- **Time Series Analysis:**
  - Time series analysis is vital in financial modeling, as it deals with data points ordered in time. Techniques include moving averages, autoregressive integrated moving average (ARIMA) models, and seasonal decomposition.
  - This method is particularly useful for analyzing stock prices, economic indicators, and interest rates, which are inherently time-dependent.

Pitfalls

- **Overfitting:**
  - Overfitting occurs when a model is too finely tuned to the specifics of the historical data, making it great at predicting the past but poor at forecasting the future. This is a common issue with complex models, such as deep learning models.
  - Avoiding overfitting requires careful model validation and testing, including techniques like cross-validation and regularization.
- **Data Quality Issues:**
  - The accuracy of any predictive model is heavily reliant on the quality of the input data. Issues such as missing values, outliers, or incorrect data can significantly skew results.
  - Ensuring high data quality involves rigorous data

cleaning, validation, and sometimes data imputation techniques.

- **Ignoring Market Regime Changes:**
  - Financial markets are influenced by numerous factors, including economic cycles, policy changes, and geopolitical events. Models that do not account for these regime changes can become outdated.
  - Adaptive models that can recognize and adjust to different market regimes are crucial. This might involve incorporating macroeconomic variables or using dynamic models that evolve with the data.

In summary, while predictive models are indispensable tools in the modern financial landscape, their effectiveness is contingent upon the application of appropriate techniques and the avoidance of common pitfalls. A comprehensive understanding of both aspects is crucial for advanced investors seeking to harness the power of predictive modeling in their investment strategies.

Techniques in Building Predictive Models

Predictive modeling in finance is a sophisticated process that involves various techniques ranging from traditional statistical methods to advanced machine learning algorithms. These techniques are crucial for understanding market behaviors and forecasting future trends. Here's a closer look at each:

Statistical Analysis and Econometrics

- **Statistical Methods:**
    - Fundamental to predictive modeling, these methods involve analyzing historical financial data to identify trends and patterns.
    - Common techniques include regression analysis, which assesses the relationship between variables; hypothesis testing, which tests assumptions about data; and variance analysis, which explores the spread of data points.
- **Econometrics:**
    - This field marries economic theory with statistical methods, providing a more nuanced approach to analyzing financial data.
    - Econometrics allows for the construction of models that not only analyze historical relationships but also incorporate economic principles, making predictions more grounded in economic reality.

Machine Learning Algorithms

- **Learning from Historical Data:**
    - Machine learning algorithms can process vast datasets and extract patterns that might be invisible to traditional analyses.

    - These include supervised learning models like linear and logistic regression for prediction and classification tasks, respectively, and unsupervised learning models like clustering, which can identify natural groupings in data.
- **Deep Learning:**
    - A more complex subset of machine learning, deep learning utilizes neural networks to model and forecast financial phenomena.
    - Deep learning is particularly potent for handling large-scale, complex datasets with numerous variables, making it suitable for intricate financial market forecasting.

Time Series Analysis

- **Analysis of Time-Ordered Data Points:**
    - Essential in financial modeling, this technique analyzes data points that are chronologically ordered, such as daily stock prices or monthly interest rates.
    - It involves methods like moving averages, which smooth out short-term fluctuations; ARIMA models, which are used to forecast future points in a series; and seasonal decomposition, which identifies and adjusts for seasonal patterns in time series data.
- **Applicability in Finance:**
    - Time series analysis is particularly useful for studying financial instruments like stocks, bonds, and derivatives, whose values change over time.
    - This method is valuable for understanding

historical trends, cyclicality, and seasonal effects in financial markets.

These techniques, when skillfully applied, provide a comprehensive toolkit for investors and analysts looking to build predictive models in finance. The key is to choose the right technique based on the specific characteristics of the data and the forecasting objectives, and to remain cognizant of the underlying assumptions and limitations of each method.

Pitfalls in Building Predictive Models

While predictive models are invaluable tools in finance, several pitfalls can undermine their effectiveness. Recognizing and addressing these pitfalls is crucial for developing reliable and robust models.

Overfitting

- **Problem Description:**
    - Overfitting is a common challenge, especially with complex models such as those in deep learning. It occurs when a model becomes too attuned to the idiosyncrasies of the training data, capturing noise as if it were a genuine signal.
    - This results in a model that performs exceptionally well on historical data but fails to generalize to new, unseen data.
- **Mitigation Strategies:**
    - **Model Validation and Testing:** Regularly validating the model against a set of data not used in training (like a validation or test set) is essential to check for overfitting.
    - **Cross-Validation:** This technique involves dividing the data into subsets and using these subsets to train and test the model multiple times. It helps in assessing the model's ability to generalize.
    - **Regularization:** Techniques like L1 and L2 regularization can penalize overly complex models, thus reducing the risk of overfitting.

Data Quality Issues

- **Impact on Model Accuracy:**
    - The quality of input data is paramount in predictive modeling. Poor data quality, including

issues like missing values, outliers, or incorrect data, can lead to misleading results and poor model performance.

- **Ensuring Data Integrity:**
  - **Data Cleaning:** This involves processes like identifying and correcting errors, filling in missing values, and smoothing out noise.
  - **Data Validation:** Ensuring that data is accurate, relevant, and consistent before it is used in model training.
  - **Data Imputation Techniques:** In cases where data is missing, techniques such as mean imputation, regression imputation, or more advanced methods can be used to estimate missing values.

Ignoring Market Regime Changes

- **Relevance to Financial Markets:**
  - Financial markets are dynamic, influenced by a myriad of factors including economic cycles, policy changes, and geopolitical events. Models that don't account for changes in these underlying regimes can become quickly outdated.
- **Adapting to Market Dynamics:**
  - **Incorporating Macroeconomic Variables:** Including variables that capture broader economic and market shifts can make models more resilient to changes in market regimes.
  - **Dynamic Modeling:** Developing models that can adapt and evolve with changing market conditions. This may involve techniques like rolling window analysis or adaptive algorithms that update themselves as new data becomes available.

In conclusion, building predictive models in finance requires not only a deep understanding of various modeling techniques but also an awareness of potential pitfalls. Overfitting, data quality issues, and ignoring market regime changes are significant challenges that must be addressed to ensure the creation of effective and reliable financial models. By implementing rigorous validation, data management, and adaptive modeling techniques, these pitfalls can be mitigated, leading to more accurate and robust predictive models.

2.2 High-Frequency Trading: Opportunities and Risks

High-Frequency Trading (HFT) is a method of trading that uses powerful computer programs to transact a large number of orders at extremely high speeds. While it offers significant opportunities, it also comes with substantial risks.

Opportunities

- **Arbitrage Opportunities:**
    - HFT allows traders to capitalize on price discrepancies across different markets or securities, often existing for mere fractions of a second. These arbitrage opportunities can include statistical arbitrage, index arbitrage, or triangular arbitrage in foreign exchange markets.
    - By exploiting these price differences, HFT firms can secure profits from small price gaps that might be too fleeting for human traders to exploit.
- **Market Making:**
    - HFT firms often act as market makers, providing liquidity to the markets by continuously buying and selling securities.
    - This activity can earn them small profits on the bid-ask spread, contributing to more efficient and liquid markets.

- **Speed:**
  - The ability to execute orders at incredibly high speeds is a significant advantage of HFT. This speed allows HFT firms to act on market information and trading opportunities much faster than traditional traders.
  - Speed in trading can also facilitate faster price discovery in the markets, leading to more accurate and current market prices.

Risks

- **Market Impact and Instability:**
  - While providing liquidity, HFT can also contribute to increased market volatility and sudden market swings, especially during times of stress or uncertainty.
  - Flash crashes, like the one in May 2010, have been partly attributed to the dynamics of high-frequency trading.
- **Systemic Risks:**
  - The interconnectedness of financial markets means that errors or anomalies in high-frequency trading systems can propagate quickly, potentially causing significant market disruptions.
  - Algorithmic glitches, unintended interactions of different trading algorithms, or extreme market conditions can trigger systemic risks.
- **Regulatory and Ethical Considerations:**
  - There is ongoing scrutiny and debate regarding the impact of HFT on market fairness and integrity. Critics argue that HFT can create an

uneven playing field and might lead to market manipulation.

- Regulatory bodies in various countries are continuously evaluating and updating rules to address the challenges posed by HFT, focusing on ensuring market stability and fairness.

In conclusion, High-Frequency Trading represents a double-edged sword in modern financial markets. While it offers substantial opportunities through arbitrage, market making, and the speed of execution, it also poses risks related to market stability, systemic impacts, and regulatory challenges. As financial technology continues to evolve, the balance between leveraging the benefits of HFT and mitigating its risks remains a pivotal concern for market participants and regulators alike.

Opportunities in High-Frequency Trading (HFT)

High-Frequency Trading (HFT) leverages advanced technology to execute rapid trades in financial markets, offering unique opportunities that were not feasible in traditional trading methodologies. These opportunities are primarily driven by the ability to quickly analyze and act upon market data.

Arbitrage Opportunities

- **Exploiting Price Discrepancies:**
    - HFT enables traders to identify and capitalize on price discrepancies that exist momentarily across different markets or securities. This includes sophisticated strategies like statistical arbitrage, index arbitrage, and triangular arbitrage in foreign exchange markets.
    - These opportunities often exist for a fraction of a second and would be virtually impossible to exploit without the speed and automated analysis capabilities of HFT.
- **Securing Profits from Market Inefficiencies:**
    - By quickly acting on these small price gaps, HFT firms can secure profits that, while small on a per-transaction basis, can accumulate to significant amounts due to the volume of trades.

Market Making

- **Providing Market Liquidity:**
    - HFT firms frequently engage in market-making activities, constantly buying and selling securities, thereby providing liquidity to the markets.
    - This continuous flow of transactions helps reduce bid-ask spreads and makes it easier for other

market participants to trade, contributing to overall market efficiency.

- **Profiting from Bid-Ask Spreads:**
    - HFT firms earn profits from the small differences between the buying and selling prices (the bid-ask spread), benefiting from the large volume of trades they conduct.

Speed

- **Rapid Execution of Trades:**
    - The hallmark of HFT is the ability to execute orders at speeds incomprehensible to human traders. This rapid execution allows HFT firms to act on market information and opportunities swiftly.
    - The speed advantage is a crucial factor in the success of HFT, allowing these firms to be the first to act on new market information.
- **Enhancing Price Discovery:**
    - The fast-paced trading of HFT can facilitate quicker price discovery in the markets. This leads to more accurate and current market pricing, which can be beneficial for the overall market by reflecting information and changes in market conditions more rapidly.

In summary, the opportunities presented by High-Frequency Trading are mainly rooted in its speed and technological prowess, enabling HFT firms to exploit market inefficiencies, provide liquidity, and enhance price discovery. However, it is crucial to balance these opportunities with the understanding of the risks and broader market implications associated with HFT practices.

Risks in High-Frequency Trading (HFT)

High-Frequency Trading, while presenting significant opportunities, also carries a range of risks. These risks not only affect the firms engaging in HFT but can also have broader implications for the financial markets as a whole.

Market Impact and Instability

- **Volatility and Market Swings:**
    - One of the critical concerns of HFT is its contribution to increased market volatility. The rapid trading activities, while providing liquidity, can also lead to significant market swings, particularly in times of uncertainty or stress.
    - HFT can amplify price movements, both upward and downward, leading to heightened market volatility.
- **Flash Crashes:**
    - Events like the Flash Crash of May 2010, where the Dow Jones Industrial Average experienced a sudden and dramatic drop, have been partly attributed to HFT. These crashes occur within minutes or even seconds, driven by the high speed and volume of trades characteristic of HFT.

Systemic Risks

- **Interconnected Market Risks:**
    - The financial markets are highly interconnected, and as such, errors or anomalies in HFT systems can have a cascading effect, leading to broader market disruptions.
    - Issues such as algorithmic glitches or the unintended interactions of different trading

algorithms can trigger systemic risks that impact the stability of the financial markets.

- **Sensitivity to Extreme Conditions:**
    - In extreme market conditions, the automated nature of HFT can exacerbate market movements. For instance, a large number of sell orders triggered algorithmically can lead to sharp price declines, creating a feedback loop that further destabilizes the market.

Regulatory and Ethical Considerations

- **Market Fairness Concerns:**
    - There is ongoing debate about the fairness of HFT in the financial markets. Critics argue that HFT firms have an unfair advantage due to their speed and access to advanced technology, which can lead to an uneven playing field.
    - Concerns about market manipulation have also been raised, with HFT capabilities potentially being used to influence market prices artificially.
- **Regulatory Response:**
    - Regulatory bodies worldwide are continuously examining the impacts of HFT and updating rules to mitigate its risks. These regulations aim to ensure market stability, prevent manipulative practices, and maintain a fair trading environment for all market participants.
    - Measures such as transaction taxes, minimum order life spans, or stricter reporting requirements are among the tools regulators use to manage the risks associated with HFT.

In summary, while High-Frequency Trading offers distinct advantages in terms of speed and efficiency, it also poses risks that need to be carefully managed. These risks include market instability, systemic vulnerabilities, and concerns about fairness and regulatory compliance. As the financial landscape evolves, so does the need for ongoing assessment and management of the risks associated with advanced trading practices like HFT.

2.3 Machine Learning in Investment Decision Making

Machine learning (ML) has become an indispensable tool in the arsenal of modern investment strategies. Its ability to analyze vast amounts of data and identify patterns that might not be visible to the human eye makes it particularly valuable in financial decision-making. However, effectively leveraging ML in investment requires understanding its applications as well as acknowledging the inherent challenges and considerations.

Application

- **Pattern Recognition:**
    - ML algorithms excel at identifying complex patterns in large datasets. In financial markets, this can mean detecting subtle trends or correlations in market data that could be indicative of future price movements.
    - Techniques like clustering or classification are used to identify patterns and categorize data in meaningful ways.
- **Predictive Analytics:**
    - Utilizing historical market data, ML models can be trained to forecast future market trends or asset price movements. Regression models, for instance, can predict continuous outcomes (like future

    prices), while classification models might be used to predict binary outcomes (like market direction).
  - Predictive analytics can encompass a wide range of financial data, including economic indicators, company performance metrics, and market indices.
- **Sentiment Analysis:**
  - ML algorithms, particularly natural language processing (NLP) models, are used to analyze text data from news articles, social media, and financial reports to gauge market sentiment.
  - Sentiment analysis can provide insights into how public perception or news events might impact market movements or individual stock prices.

Challenges and Considerations

- **Interpretability:**
  - Many ML models, especially more complex ones like deep learning networks, can be seen as 'black boxes.' This means their decision-making process is not easily understandable, which can be a significant issue when transparency and understanding of investment decisions are required.
  - Efforts are ongoing in the field of ML to improve model interpretability, including techniques that provide insights into how models arrive at their decisions.
- **Data Overfitting:**
  - ML models are prone to overfitting, where they

perform well on training data but poorly on unseen data. This is often due to the model being too complex and capturing noise as if it were a signal.
    - To combat overfitting, methods like cross-validation, regularization, and ensuring a robust and diverse dataset for training are essential.
- **Dynamic Markets:**
    - Financial markets are not static; they are influenced by a myriad of factors that are constantly in flux. ML models that were accurate at one time may quickly become obsolete if they don't adapt to changing market conditions.
    - Continual retraining and updating of models with new data, and incorporating adaptive learning techniques, are crucial to maintain the relevance and accuracy of ML-based investment strategies.

Incorporating machine learning into investment decision-making offers the promise of enhanced analysis and predictive capabilities. However, it also necessitates a careful approach to model construction, validation, and maintenance, ensuring that these advanced tools remain effective and relevant in the fast-paced and ever-changing world of finance.

Application of Machine Learning in Investment Decision Making

Machine Learning (ML) has revolutionized the field of investment decision-making by providing powerful tools to analyze and interpret vast amounts of financial data. Here's a closer look at the key applications of ML in this domain:

Pattern Recognition

- **Detecting Complex Patterns:**
    - ML algorithms are adept at sifting through large and complex datasets to uncover patterns that might be invisible to traditional analysis. This capability is particularly valuable in financial markets, where subtle trends and correlations can have significant implications.
    - For instance, an algorithm might identify a recurring pattern in stock price movements related to specific economic announcements or market events.
- **Clustering and Classification:**
    - Techniques such as clustering help in grouping similar data points together, thereby identifying underlying patterns in market behavior. Classification algorithms categorize data into different classes based on learned patterns, which can be useful in decision-making processes like identifying bullish or bearish market trends.

Predictive Analytics

- **Forecasting Market Trends:**
    - ML models, especially regression models, are used to predict future market trends or asset price

movements based on historical data. These predictions can be about price levels, stock movements, or market direction.
    - Predictive analytics in finance includes forecasting stock prices, bond yields, commodity prices, and even macroeconomic indicators.
- **Diverse Financial Data Analysis:**
    - The scope of predictive analytics in finance is broad, encompassing various types of financial data such as historical price data, economic indicators, company earnings reports, and market indices. The integration of these diverse data types can lead to more accurate and comprehensive market predictions.

Sentiment Analysis

- **Analyzing Text Data:**
    - ML, particularly NLP models, are increasingly used to analyze textual data sources like news articles, social media posts, and financial reports to assess market sentiment.
    - This form of analysis can identify the general mood or opinion of investors and the public towards certain markets or specific stocks, which can be an indicator of future market movements.
- **Impact of Public Perception:**
    - Sentiment analysis can reveal how public perception and news events might influence market movements or the performance of individual stocks. For instance, positive news about a company's innovation could lead to an

uptick in its stock price, a trend that sentiment analysis can help predict.

In summary, the application of machine learning in investment decision-making spans from pattern recognition and predictive analytics to sentiment analysis, each playing a crucial role in interpreting market data and trends. These advanced techniques offer investors and analysts a more refined and data-driven approach to understanding and predicting market behavior. However, the effective use of ML in finance requires not only technical expertise but also a nuanced understanding of the market dynamics and the data being analyzed.

Challenges and Considerations in Machine Learning for Investment Decision Making

While machine learning (ML) offers tremendous potential in financial analysis and prediction, several challenges and considerations must be addressed to ensure its effective application. These challenges stem from the complexities of ML models, the quality of data they are trained on, and the dynamic nature of financial markets.

Interpretability

- **Complex Models as 'Black Boxes':**
  - One of the significant issues with advanced ML models, particularly deep learning networks, is their lack of interpretability. Often referred to as 'black boxes,' these models make decisions or predictions that are not easily understood by humans. This lack of transparency can be problematic in investment decision-making where understanding the rationale behind decisions is crucial.
- **Improving Model Interpretability:**
  - Efforts are being made in the ML community to enhance the interpretability of complex models. This includes techniques like feature importance analysis, which helps to understand which aspects of the data are driving the model's predictions, and model visualization methods that offer insights into the inner workings of neural networks.

Data Overfitting

- **Risk of Overfitting:**

- ◦ ML models are susceptible to overfitting, particularly when they are too complex relative to the amount and quality of the training data. Overfitting occurs when a model learns the noise in the training data instead of the underlying pattern, leading to poor performance on new, unseen data.
- **Mitigation Techniques:**
    - To prevent overfitting, various strategies are employed. Cross-validation, where the data is split into multiple parts for training and validation, helps in assessing the model's ability to generalize. Regularization techniques can penalize model complexity, encouraging simpler models that are less likely to overfit. Ensuring a robust and diverse training dataset is also crucial.

Dynamic Markets

- **Constantly Changing Markets:**
    - Financial markets are inherently dynamic, influenced by a wide range of ever-changing factors including economic indicators, political events, and market sentiment. This means that ML models trained on historical data might not perform well in the future if the market conditions change significantly.
- **Need for Continual Learning:**
    - To remain effective, ML models need regular updates and retraining with new data. Adaptive learning techniques, which allow models to evolve with changing market conditions, can be

particularly valuable. This might include using online learning approaches where models are continuously updated, or retraining models at regular intervals with new data.

In conclusion, while machine learning holds great promise for enhancing investment strategies, its successful application requires careful consideration of model interpretability, the risk of data overfitting, and the dynamic nature of financial markets. Addressing these challenges is essential for building reliable, effective, and transparent ML-based investment tools.

Chapter 3: Alternative Investments and Unconventional Assets

In the evolving landscape of investment, alternative investments and unconventional assets have become increasingly important for diversification and potential returns. This chapter explores the nuances of these investment classes, offering insights into their unique characteristics and the strategies required for successful navigation.

3.1 Navigating Private Equity and Venture Capital

- **Understanding Private Equity (PE):**
    - PE involves investing in companies not listed on public stock exchanges. It often entails buying stakes in mature, private or public companies, with the aim of restructuring or improving performance before a subsequent exit, typically through a sale or an IPO.
    - Key strategies include leveraged buyouts, growth capital, and distressed investments.
- **Venture Capital (VC) Dynamics:**
    - VC focuses on investing in early-stage, high-potential startups. The risk profile is typically higher than PE due to the nascent stage of the companies.
    - Investors in VC often provide not just capital but

also mentorship and strategic guidance to help these startups grow.

- **Risk and Reward Considerations:**
    - Both PE and VC investments carry significant risk, including illiquidity, reliance on management teams, and market risks. However, they can also offer substantial rewards, including high returns and the potential for significant influence over portfolio companies.

3.2 Investing in Real Assets: Real Estate, Infrastructure, and Commodities

- **Real Estate Investments:**
    - Investing in real estate encompasses a range of strategies, from direct property acquisitions to investing in real estate investment trusts (REITs). Real estate can offer stable cash flows (rents), potential appreciation, and a hedge against inflation.
- **Infrastructure Investments:**
    - Infrastructure investing involves assets that provide essential services, such as transportation systems, utilities, and communication networks. These investments often provide long-term, stable cash flows, and can be less sensitive to economic cycles.
- **Commodities as an Asset Class:**
    - Commodities include physical goods like oil, gold, and agricultural products. Investing in commodities can provide diversification, act as an inflation hedge, and offer unique return

opportunities. However, they also come with high volatility and can be influenced by complex factors like geopolitical events and environmental conditions.

3.3 Cryptocurrencies and Blockchain Technology Investments

- **The Rise of Cryptocurrencies:**
    - Cryptocurrencies have emerged as a new asset class, offering decentralization, potential high returns, and a new technology paradigm. The market is characterized by high volatility and is influenced by factors like technology developments, regulatory changes, and market sentiment.
- **Blockchain Technology:**
    - Beyond cryptocurrencies, blockchain technology presents investment opportunities in various sectors through its potential to disrupt traditional business models. This includes areas like supply chain management, financial services, and digital identity.
- **Risk Assessment and Regulatory Landscape:**
    - Investments in cryptocurrencies and blockchain technology carry unique risks, including regulatory uncertainty, technological risks, and market adoption challenges. It's essential for investors to understand these risks and the evolving regulatory landscape.

This chapter on alternative investments and unconventional assets provides a comprehensive overview for investors looking to diversify into these less traditional areas. Understanding the unique characteristics, risks, and opportunities of these assets is crucial for developing a well-rounded and robust investment portfolio.

3.1 Navigating Private Equity and Venture Capital

Understanding Private Equity (PE)

- **Investment in Non-Public Companies:**
    - Private Equity involves investment in companies that are not listed on public stock exchanges. This includes a range of activities from buying stakes in mature, private companies to taking public companies private.
- **Strategies Employed in PE:**
    - **Leveraged Buyouts (LBOs):** Involves buying a company primarily through debt financing, aiming to improve its value and performance for a profitable exit.
    - **Growth Capital:** Investment in relatively mature companies that are looking for capital to expand or restructure operations, enter new markets, or finance a significant acquisition without a change of control.
    - **Distressed Investments:** Focuses on buying assets in troubled companies at a discounted price, often aiming to turn them around or sell them for a profit.

Venture Capital (VC) Dynamics

- **Investing in Early-Stage Startups:**

    - Venture Capital is the infusion of funds into early-stage, high-potential startups. VC is known for its high-risk and high-reward nature due to the nascent stage and unproven models of the target companies.
- **Beyond Capital: Mentorship and Guidance:**
    - VC investors typically offer more than just capital; they provide strategic guidance, mentorship, industry connections, and operational expertise to help startups scale and succeed.

Risk and Reward Considerations

- **Navigating Risks:**
    - Both PE and VC investments are inherently risky. The risks include illiquidity (as the investment is locked in for several years), reliance on the success of the management teams, and broader market risks.
    - In VC, the risk is accentuated due to the early and unproven stage of the businesses. Many startups fail to deliver expected returns, leading to a high loss rate.
- **Potential for High Returns:**
    - Despite the risks, both PE and VC can offer substantial rewards. Successful investments in these spaces can yield significantly higher returns compared to traditional equity markets.
    - In addition to financial returns, PE and VC investments offer the opportunity for significant influence and control over portfolio companies,

which can be a strategic advantage for investors.

Private Equity and Venture Capital represent sophisticated, high-risk, and potentially high-reward areas of the investment universe. They require deep due diligence, a strong understanding of market dynamics, and patience for long-term value creation. For advanced investors, PE and VC offer unique opportunities to invest in and shape the growth of companies, from fledgling startups to established private firms.

Understanding Private Equity (PE)

Private Equity (PE) represents a critical segment of the investment landscape, offering unique opportunities and strategies distinct from public market investments. It involves deploying capital into companies that are not publicly traded on stock exchanges, encompassing various investment strategies and objectives.

Investment in Non-Public Companies

- **Scope of Investment:**
    - PE firms invest in a wide array of companies, ranging from mature, private businesses to public companies that are taken private. This flexibility allows PE firms to target companies at different stages of their life cycle and with varying growth prospects.
- **Nature of Investment:**
    - Investments in these companies are typically long-term in nature, with PE firms actively involved in the management and strategic direction of the company to enhance value over time.
    - The exit strategies for these investments can include selling the company to another firm (private sale), an Initial Public Offering (IPO), or selling to another PE firm.

Strategies Employed in PE

- **Leveraged Buyouts (LBOs):**
    - LBOs are a prevalent strategy in PE, involving the acquisition of a company predominantly through debt financing. The acquired company's assets often serve as collateral for the loans.

    - Post-acquisition, the focus is on improving the company's value and performance to eventually exit the investment profitably, typically after restructuring debts and improving operational efficiencies.
- **Growth Capital:**
    - This strategy focuses on investing in relatively mature companies that require capital to expand operations, enter new markets, restructure their operations, or finance significant acquisitions.
    - Unlike LBOs, growth capital investments don't usually entail a change of control in the company but rather are aimed at facilitating expansion and scaling of operations.
- **Distressed Investments:**
    - Distressed investments involve buying assets or stakes in financially troubled companies at a discount. The goal is often to turn around the company's fortunes and sell the assets or the entire company at a profit.
    - This strategy requires a deep understanding of the reasons behind a company's distress and the potential pathways for recovery and value creation.

In summary, Private Equity encompasses a range of investment strategies targeting non-public companies, each with its unique risk-reward profile. From leveraged buyouts to growth capital and distressed investments, PE offers investors the opportunity to directly influence the trajectory of a company and realize value through strategic, operational, and financial improvements. The success in PE investing hinges on the selection of the right companies, effective management strategies, and timing of entry and exit.

Venture Capital (VC) Dynamics

Venture Capital (VC) plays a pivotal role in the entrepreneurial ecosystem, fueling innovation and growth in the early stages of startup development. The dynamics of VC are characterized by a unique blend of high risk and potential for substantial rewards, along with an active involvement in the nurturing and growth of the invested companies.

Investing in Early-Stage Startups

- **Targeting High-Potential Startups:**
  - VC firms specialize in investing in early-stage companies with high growth potential. These startups are often in the initial phases of their development, where they are working on developing a product or service, gaining market traction, or scaling their operations.
- **High-Risk, High-Reward Nature:**
  - The investment in these nascent companies is inherently risky, as many startups fail to materialize their potential. The risks are augmented due to unproven business models, uncertain market acceptance, and the challenges of scaling a business.
  - Despite the risks, successful investments in startups can yield significant returns. A small stake in a startup can grow exponentially in value if the company becomes successful, as seen in numerous tech industry success stories.

Beyond Capital: Mentorship and Guidance

- **Providing More Than Funding:**
  - VC investors often bring much more to the table

than just financial investment. They play an active role in the development of their portfolio companies.
    - This involvement includes providing strategic guidance, helping refine business models, advising on key hires, and assisting in crucial business decisions.
- **Leveraging Industry Connections:**
    - VC firms typically have extensive networks in various industries and can leverage these connections to benefit their portfolio companies. This can include introductions to potential customers, partners, or even future investors.
- **Operational Expertise:**
    - Many VC firms or individual investors bring in their operational expertise, gleaned from years of experience in specific industries or in building and scaling companies. This expertise can be invaluable for startup founders who might be navigating these challenges for the first time.

In essence, Venture Capital is not just about injecting funds into early-stage companies; it's about actively participating in the journey of turning innovative ideas into successful businesses. This active involvement is a hallmark of VC and sets it apart from other forms of investment. The combination of capital, expertise, and network that VC firms provide can be a crucial catalyst for startup growth and success.

Risk and Reward Considerations in Private Equity and Venture Capital

Investing in Private Equity (PE) and Venture Capital (VC) encompasses a unique blend of risks and potential rewards. These investment strategies diverge significantly from traditional equity investments, primarily due to their illiquid nature, high reliance on management teams, and the inherent risks of the businesses they invest in.

Navigating Risks

- **Illiquidity:**
  - Both PE and VC investments are characteristically illiquid. The capital invested is typically locked in for several years, sometimes even a decade or more. This long-term commitment means investors cannot easily convert these investments into cash without a significant exit event like a sale or IPO.
- **Dependence on Management Teams:**
  - The success of PE and VC investments heavily relies on the capabilities and performance of the management teams of the portfolio companies. Ineffective management can lead to underperformance and even failure of the investment.
- **Market Risks and Business Stage:**
  - Broader market risks, such as economic downturns or sector-specific challenges, can impact the performance of these investments.
  - In VC, particularly, the risk is amplified due to the early and often unproven stage of the businesses. The high failure rate of startups means that while

some investments may yield high returns, many may result in losses.

Potential for High Returns

- **Substantial Rewards:**
  - Despite the high risks, successful investments in PE and VC can offer significant rewards. Returns from these investments can far exceed those from traditional equity markets, especially if a startup becomes highly successful or a PE turnaround strategy works well.
- **Influence and Control:**
  - Investors in PE and VC often obtain significant influence over the operations and strategic direction of the companies they invest in. This control can be a strategic advantage, allowing investors to steer companies towards growth and success.
- **Diversification Benefits:**
  - PE and VC provide diversification away from standard market risks associated with traditional equity and bond investments. Their performance is often not directly correlated with public markets, adding a layer of diversification to an investment portfolio.

In summary, while PE and VC investments carry inherent risks, including illiquidity, high reliance on management, and susceptibility to market and business stage risks, they also offer the potential for substantial returns. These returns are not just financial; they also include the opportunity for significant influence over the direction and success of the investee companies. For investors willing to undertake these risks and actively engage with their investments, PE and VC can be rewarding components of a diversified investment strategy.

3.2 Investing in Real Assets: Real Estate, Infrastructure, and Commodities

Real Estate Investments

- **Diverse Investment Strategies:**
    - Real estate investment is multifaceted, ranging from direct property purchases (like residential or commercial properties) to indirect investments through Real Estate Investment Trusts (REITs).
    - Direct property investment involves buying, managing, and selling physical properties. REITs, on the other hand, allow investors to buy shares in companies that own and manage a portfolio of real estate assets.
- **Benefits of Real Estate:**
    - Real estate can provide stable cash flows, primarily through rents, making it an attractive option for income-seeking investors.
    - There's also the potential for capital appreciation as property values increase over time.
    - Real estate is often viewed as a hedge against inflation since property values and rents typically increase with inflation.

Infrastructure Investments

- **Investing in Essential Services:**
    - Infrastructure investment entails funding assets that provide essential services – such as transportation systems (like highways and airports), utilities (energy, water), and communication networks.
    - These investments are often capital-intensive and have long lifecycles, making them suitable for long-term investors.
- **Stability and Economic Insensitivity:**
    - Infrastructure assets generally provide long-term, stable cash flows, often backed by regulatory frameworks or long-term contracts.
    - These investments can be less sensitive to economic cycles, as the demand for essential services tends to be consistent regardless of economic conditions.

Commodities as an Asset Class

- **Diverse Range of Physical Goods:**
    - Commodities as an investment class include physical goods like oil, gold, agricultural products, and metals. These can be traded on commodities exchanges or invested in indirectly through commodity-focused funds or ETFs.
- **Characteristics of Commodity Investments:**
    - Commodities can offer portfolio diversification, as their prices are often driven by different factors than those affecting stock and bond markets.
    - They can act as an inflation hedge since

commodity prices typically rise with inflation.
    - However, commodities are known for their high price volatility, influenced by a range of factors including geopolitical events, environmental conditions, and changes in supply and demand dynamics.

In summary, investing in real assets such as real estate, infrastructure, and commodities provides investors with opportunities for stable cash flows, inflation hedging, and portfolio diversification. Each of these asset classes comes with its own set of characteristics, benefits, and risks, making them important considerations for a diversified investment strategy. Real estate offers income through rents and potential appreciation, infrastructure investments provide stable cash flows and are often economically insensitive, and commodities offer inflation hedging but with higher volatility. Understanding the nuances of each asset class is crucial for investors looking to navigate the world of real assets effectively.

Real Estate Investments

Real estate investments stand as a cornerstone in the landscape of alternative investments, offering a diversity of strategies and a range of benefits. Whether through direct property acquisition or indirect methods such as REITs, real estate presents unique opportunities for investors.

Diverse Investment Strategies

- **Direct Property Investment:**
    - Involves the acquisition, management, and sale of physical properties. This can include various types of real estate, such as residential (houses, apartments), commercial (office buildings, retail spaces), or industrial (warehouses, manufacturing facilities).
    - Direct investment allows for greater control over the asset, including decisions related to leasing, renovations, and sale timings.
- **Investing Through REITs:**
    - Real Estate Investment Trusts (REITs) offer a way to invest in real estate indirectly. REITs are companies that own, operate, or finance income-producing real estate across a range of property sectors.
    - Investing in REITs allows individuals to buy shares in these companies, making it possible to invest in real estate without having to buy or manage the property directly. REITs are typically known for providing dividend income to investors.

Benefits of Real Estate

- **Stable Cash Flows:**
    - Real estate investments can generate stable cash flows, primarily through rents. This feature is particularly appealing for income-focused investors.
    - The stability of rental income, especially in well-located properties or in sectors with strong demand, adds a layer of security to the investment.
- **Capital Appreciation:**
    - Over time, real estate properties often appreciate in value, offering the potential for capital gains upon sale.
    - The rate of appreciation can vary significantly based on factors like location, property type, market conditions, and how the property is managed.
- **Inflation Hedge:**
    - Real estate is often considered a good hedge against inflation. As inflation rises, so typically do property values and rents, helping to protect the purchasing power of the investment.
    - This characteristic is particularly important in inflationary environments or as a long-term strategy to preserve wealth.

In essence, real estate investment offers a tangible asset with the potential for both income generation and capital appreciation, making it a valuable component of a diversified investment portfolio. Its ability to provide stable cash flows, potential for appreciation, and protection against inflation are key attributes that attract investors. However, like all investments, real estate also carries risks and requires due diligence, market knowledge, and effective management to realize its full potential.

Infrastructure Investments

Infrastructure investments represent a key segment in the realm of alternative investments, focusing on assets that are fundamental to the functioning of societies and economies. These investments typically involve substantial capital and are characterized by their long-term nature.

Investing in Essential Services

- **Scope of Infrastructure Assets:**
    - Infrastructure investments cover a wide array of assets that provide essential services. This includes transportation infrastructure like highways, airports, and ports; utilities such as energy (electricity and gas) and water; and communication infrastructure like broadband networks.
    - These assets play a critical role in economic development and societal well-being, making them vital and often indispensable.
- **Capital-Intensive with Long Lifecycles:**
    - Investing in infrastructure is typically capital-intensive, involving significant upfront costs. However, these assets usually have long lifecycles, often spanning several decades.
    - The long-term nature of these investments makes them particularly suitable for investors with a long investment horizon, such as pension funds or institutional investors.

Stability and Economic Insensitivity

- **Long-Term, Stable Cash Flows:**
    - Infrastructure investments are known for

providing stable and predictable cash flows. This stability often comes from the essential nature of the services provided and, in many cases, is further supported by regulatory frameworks or long-term contracts.
    - For example, toll roads or regulated utilities can generate consistent revenue streams, providing a steady return on investment.
- **Resilience to Economic Fluctuations:**
    - The demand for essential infrastructure services tends to remain stable, making these investments less sensitive to economic cycles. For instance, regardless of the economic climate, there is a continuous need for energy, water, and transportation.
    - This characteristic can provide a buffer for investment portfolios during economic downturns, adding a layer of security against market volatility.

Infrastructure investments offer a compelling proposition for investors seeking stable, long-term returns and lower correlation with economic cycles. The essential nature of the services provided by infrastructure assets underpins their stability and resilience, making them an attractive option for diversifying investment portfolios. However, the capital-intensive nature and complexity of these assets require thorough due diligence, understanding of regulatory environments, and often, a longer investment horizon.

Commodities as an Asset Class

Commodities represent a distinct category in the investment world, encompassing a wide range of physical goods. Their unique characteristics and market dynamics offer specific advantages and challenges for investors, making them a noteworthy consideration for portfolio diversification.

Diverse Range of Physical Goods

- **Types of Commodities:**
    - The commodities market includes a variety of physical goods, such as energy sources (like oil and natural gas), precious metals (such as gold and silver), industrial metals (like copper and aluminum), and agricultural products (including grains, coffee, and sugar).
    - These commodities are essential for various industries and everyday life, making them fundamental economic building blocks.
- **Ways to Invest:**
    - Commodities can be traded on exchanges, where they are bought and sold in standardized contracts. This direct method is more common among professional traders due to the complexities and specifics of commodity markets.
    - For individual investors, indirect investment options are available, such as commodity-focused mutual funds or exchange-traded funds (ETFs). These funds invest in a basket of commodities or commodity-producing companies, providing easier access to this asset class.

Characteristics of Commodity Investments

- **Portfolio Diversification:**
    - Commodities often have a low correlation with traditional asset classes like stocks and bonds. This means that their prices may move independently of the stock and bond markets, providing a diversification benefit to an investment portfolio.
    - This diversification can help reduce overall portfolio risk and smooth out returns over time.
- **Inflation Hedging:**
    - Commodities are frequently seen as a hedge against inflation. When inflation rises, the value of commodities usually increases, as they are tangible assets with intrinsic value.
    - For example, in times of inflation, the price of gold often rises, making it a popular choice for protecting against declining purchasing power.
- **Volatility Considerations:**
    - Commodity markets are known for their high volatility. Prices can fluctuate widely due to a variety of factors, including geopolitical events, environmental conditions, and changes in supply and demand dynamics.
    - For instance, oil prices can be significantly impacted by geopolitical tensions in oil-producing regions, while agricultural commodity prices can be influenced by weather conditions.

In summary, commodities as an asset class offer opportunities for diversification and inflation hedging, but they also come with the challenge of high volatility. Their price movements are influenced by a complex interplay of global factors, making them both a potentially rewarding and risky investment. For investors considering commodities, understanding these market dynamics and the role commodities can play in a portfolio is critical.

3.3 Cryptocurrencies and Blockchain Technology Investments

The advent of cryptocurrencies and the underlying blockchain technology has introduced a novel and rapidly evolving asset class. This sector, while offering significant potential for innovation and returns, also comes with a unique set of risks and challenges that investors need to navigate carefully.

The Rise of Cryptocurrencies

- **New Asset Class Characteristics:**
  - Cryptocurrencies represent a new paradigm in the world of finance, characterized by their decentralization, digital nature, and use of blockchain technology.
  - They offer potential for high returns, which has attracted significant attention from both retail and institutional investors. Notable cryptocurrencies include Bitcoin, Ethereum, and numerous altcoins.
- **Market Volatility and Influencing Factors:**
  - The cryptocurrency market is known for its high volatility, with prices subject to rapid and significant fluctuations.
  - Price movements are influenced by various factors, including technological developments,

regulatory news, market sentiment, and broader adoption trends.

Blockchain Technology

- **Potential Beyond Currencies:**
    - Blockchain technology, the backbone of cryptocurrencies, has implications far beyond digital currencies. It presents opportunities for innovation and investment across various sectors.
    - This technology can disrupt traditional business models in areas such as supply chain management, where it can enhance transparency and efficiency, financial services with the potential for decentralized finance (DeFi), and digital identity management, ensuring secure and tamper-proof identity verification processes.

Risk Assessment and Regulatory Landscape

- **Understanding Unique Risks:**
    - Investments in cryptocurrencies and blockchain technology are fraught with unique risks. These include the nascent and evolving nature of the technology, the risk of hacking and security breaches, and significant market adoption challenges.
    - The value of cryptocurrencies can be highly speculative, and the market is still in a relatively early stage of development, leading to uncertainty and unpredictability.
- **Navigating Regulatory Uncertainty:**
    - The regulatory environment for cryptocurrencies

and blockchain technology is still developing and varies significantly across different jurisdictions. Regulatory changes can have a substantial impact on the market.

- Investors must stay informed about the regulatory landscape in various regions, as regulatory actions can influence market dynamics and the viability of certain blockchain applications.

In summary, while cryptocurrencies and blockchain technology offer exciting investment opportunities with the potential for high returns and transformative impact across industries, they also present significant risks and regulatory uncertainties. Investors venturing into this space need to conduct thorough research, stay abreast of technological and regulatory developments, and approach these investments with a clear understanding of their risk tolerance and investment horizon.

The Rise of Cryptocurrencies

New Asset Class Characteristics

- **Decentralization and Digital Nature:**
    - Cryptocurrencies have introduced a new paradigm in finance, largely defined by their decentralized nature. Unlike traditional currencies, they are not controlled by any central authority, such as a government or central bank.
    - They are purely digital, existing on blockchain technology, which allows for secure, transparent, and tamper-proof transactions. This technology underpins their operation, ensuring integrity and trust in transactions without the need for intermediaries.
- **High-Return Potential:**
    - The potential for high returns has been a significant draw for both retail and institutional investors. Cryptocurrencies like Bitcoin and Ethereum have seen substantial price increases over a relatively short period, garnering widespread attention.
    - The emergence of various altcoins (alternative cryptocurrencies to Bitcoin) has further expanded the landscape, offering diverse investment opportunities with different risk-reward profiles.

Market Volatility and Influencing Factors

- **High Volatility:**
    - The cryptocurrency market is characterized by extreme volatility. Prices can experience rapid and significant fluctuations within short time frames,

making the market both potentially lucrative and risky.
    - This volatility is partly due to the market's nascent nature and partly due to the speculative behavior of many market participants.
- **Influencing Factors:**
    - **Technological Developments:** Innovations in blockchain technology, changes in network protocols, or the introduction of new features can significantly impact cryptocurrency prices.
    - **Regulatory News:** Given the lack of clear regulatory frameworks in many regions, news of potential regulations or bans can lead to market uncertainty and price volatility.
    - **Market Sentiment:** Cryptocurrency markets are highly sensitive to investor sentiment, which can be influenced by media coverage, influencer opinions, and broader investor attitudes.
    - **Adoption Trends:** The rate and manner in which cryptocurrencies are adopted, whether by individuals, businesses, or governments, can greatly influence their value and acceptance.

In conclusion, the rise of cryptocurrencies marks a significant shift in the financial landscape, offering unique opportunities but also posing distinct challenges. The decentralized, digital nature of these assets, coupled with their potential for high returns, has captured significant investor interest. However, navigating this space requires an understanding of the inherent volatility and the complex array of factors that influence cryptocurrency markets. Investors should approach this asset class with diligence, considering both its potential and risks.

Blockchain Technology

Potential Beyond Currencies

- **Foundation for Disruption:**
    - While blockchain technology is widely recognized as the underlying mechanism of cryptocurrencies, its potential extends far beyond the realm of digital currencies. It represents a foundational technology that can revolutionize various sectors by enabling secure, transparent, and efficient transactions.
- **Sector-Wide Applications:**
    - **Supply Chain Management:** Blockchain can significantly enhance transparency and efficiency in supply chains. It enables the tracking of products from the manufacturer to the end consumer, reducing the risk of counterfeit goods and improving the traceability of raw materials.
    - **Financial Services and DeFi:** In financial services, blockchain opens the door for decentralized finance (DeFi), which operates without traditional financial intermediaries like banks. DeFi platforms can offer services ranging from lending and borrowing to insurance, all executed on blockchain networks.
    - **Digital Identity Management:** Blockchain can provide secure and tamper-proof digital identity solutions. By creating a decentralized and immutable record, individuals can have greater control and security over their digital identities, which is crucial in an increasingly digital world.

Disrupting Traditional Business Models

- **Transforming Operations:**
    - Blockchain's ability to provide a secure,

unchangeable ledger of transactions makes it suitable for transforming traditional business operations. It can streamline processes, reduce fraud, and cut operational costs.

- **Innovation Across Industries:**
    - Beyond the sectors mentioned, blockchain technology has the potential to innovate in areas like healthcare (for secure patient records), real estate (for transparent property transactions), and even in governance (for voting systems and public records).

Investment Opportunities

- **Blockchain Startups and Projects:**
    - Investment opportunities in blockchain technology manifest in various forms, including startups developing blockchain-based solutions, companies integrating blockchain into their existing operations, and projects focused on specific applications of the technology.
- **Evolving Investment Landscape:**
    - The investment landscape for blockchain technology is rapidly evolving, with venture capitalists, corporate investors, and individual investors increasingly showing interest in funding innovative blockchain projects.

Blockchain technology offers a frontier of opportunities for innovation and investment across multiple sectors, far beyond its initial application in cryptocurrencies. Its potential to disrupt traditional business models with enhanced transparency, security, and efficiency presents a fertile ground for investments that seek to capitalize on technological advancements. However, as with any emerging technology, investments in blockchain ventures require careful consideration of the technology's maturity, market readiness, and the specific use case being addressed.

Risk Assessment and Regulatory Landscape

Investing in cryptocurrencies and blockchain technology requires a comprehensive understanding of the unique risks involved and the evolving regulatory landscape. These factors play a crucial role in shaping the potential success and viability of such investments.

Understanding Unique Risks

- **Technological Risks:**
  - The technology underlying cryptocurrencies and blockchain is still nascent and evolving. While it offers groundbreaking potential, it also comes with risks like the possibility of undetected technical flaws or the challenges associated with scaling the technology.
- **Security Concerns:**
  - The risk of hacking and security breaches is a significant concern. Despite the secure nature of blockchain technology, cryptocurrency exchanges and wallets have been susceptible to high-profile hacks, leading to substantial financial losses.
- **Market Adoption and Speculation:**
  - The market for cryptocurrencies is highly speculative, and prices can be extremely volatile. This speculative nature can lead to rapid price swings based on investor sentiment rather than underlying fundamentals.
  - Market adoption challenges also persist, as widespread acceptance and use of cryptocurrencies and blockchain applications are still in the early stages.

Navigating Regulatory Uncertainty

- **Evolving Regulatory Frameworks:**
    - The regulatory landscape for cryptocurrencies and blockchain technology is in flux and varies significantly across different countries. Some jurisdictions have embraced these technologies, while others have imposed strict regulations or outright bans.
- **Impact of Regulatory Changes:**
    - Changes in regulations can have a substantial impact on the cryptocurrency market and blockchain enterprises. Regulatory decisions can influence investor confidence, market stability, and the overall growth trajectory of these technologies.
- **Staying Informed and Compliant:**
    - Investors need to stay informed about the regulatory environment in various regions, especially if they are investing internationally. Understanding these regulations is crucial to ensuring compliance and making informed investment decisions.
    - It's also important to monitor the potential for future regulatory changes, as governments and financial authorities continue to grapple with how best to regulate this dynamic and rapidly evolving space.

In summary, while cryptocurrencies and blockchain technology present new and exciting investment opportunities, they also come with unique challenges and risks. Understanding and navigating these risks, especially in the context of an uncertain regulatory environment, is crucial for investors looking to venture into this innovative yet complex domain. Caution and due diligence are key, as is staying abreast of ongoing technological advancements and regulatory developments.

Chapter 4: Behavioral Finance and Investor Psychology

In the intricate world of investing, understanding the psychological and behavioral aspects is as crucial as grasping the financial fundamentals. Chapter 4 delves into the realms of behavioral finance and investor psychology, exploring how cognitive biases, emotional discipline, and contrarian strategies play pivotal roles in investment decisions.

4.1 Cognitive Biases and Their Impact on Investment Decisions

- **Understanding Cognitive Biases:**
    - Cognitive biases are psychological tendencies that can affect decision-making processes and reasoning. In the context of investing, these biases often lead to irrational or suboptimal decisions.
    - Examples include confirmation bias (favoring information that confirms pre-existing beliefs), overconfidence bias (overestimating one's own investment abilities), and loss aversion (the tendency to prefer avoiding losses to acquiring equivalent gains).
- **Impact on Investment Choices:**
    - Cognitive biases can lead investors to make decisions that are not in line with their investment goals or risk tolerance. For instance,

    - an investor might hold onto a losing stock due to the endowment effect, valuing it more highly simply because they own it.
    - Understanding and mitigating these biases are crucial for making more rational and effective investment decisions.

4.2 Emotional Discipline in Investing

- **Role of Emotions in Investing:**
    - Emotions can play a significant role in investment decisions. Fear and greed, in particular, can drive market cycles and individual investment choices.
- **Developing Emotional Discipline:**
    - Emotional discipline involves maintaining a strategic perspective and not letting short-term market movements dictate investment decisions. This includes sticking to a well-thought-out investment plan and avoiding impulsive reactions to market volatility.
    - Techniques like setting clear investment goals, diversifying portfolios, and regularly reviewing investment strategies can help in maintaining emotional discipline.

4.3 Contrarian Investment Strategies

- **Contrarian Approach to Investing:**
    - Contrarian investing involves going against prevailing market trends or sentiment. Contrarians often buy assets when they are out of favor and sell them when they become popular.
- **Rationale and Risks:**

- The rationale behind contrarian investing is that markets can overreact to news, both positively and negatively, creating opportunities for investors who go against the grain.
- However, contrarian strategies come with risks. Timing the market can be challenging, and contrarian positions can take time to materialize into profits.

In conclusion, Chapter 4 highlights the critical interplay between psychology and investment strategies. Understanding cognitive biases and developing emotional discipline are essential for making sound investment decisions. Contrarian strategies, while potentially profitable, require a deep understanding of market dynamics and a high tolerance for risk and uncertainty. This chapter underscores the importance of a comprehensive approach that balances psychological insights with financial acumen in the pursuit of successful investing.

4.1 Cognitive Biases and Their Impact on Investment Decisions

Understanding Cognitive Biases

- **Psychological Influences on Decision-Making:**
    - Cognitive biases are ingrained psychological tendencies that affect how individuals perceive and respond to information. In investing, these biases can significantly influence decision-making, often leading to irrational or less optimal choices.
- **Common Biases in Investing:**
    - **Confirmation Bias:** This occurs when investors seek out or give more weight to information that confirms their pre-existing beliefs or hypotheses, while disregarding evidence that contradicts them.
    - **Overconfidence Bias:** Many investors overestimate their knowledge, skill, and ability to predict market movements, leading to riskier or ill-informed investment decisions.
    - **Loss Aversion:** Investors often exhibit a stronger emotional response to potential losses than to equivalent gains. This can lead to risk-averse behavior that might contradict their long-term investment goals.

Impact on Investment Choices

- **Deviation from Goals and Strategy:**
    - Cognitive biases can cause investors to make decisions that deviate from their planned investment strategy or goals. For example, an investor might sell a well-performing asset prematurely due to fear incited by market volatility, or hold onto a depreciating asset due to an emotional attachment.
- **The Endowment Effect:**
    - A specific cognitive bias relevant to investing is the endowment effect, where investors place a higher value on an asset they own compared to its market value. This can lead to holding onto losing investments longer than rational analysis would suggest.

Mitigating Cognitive Biases

- **Awareness and Education:**
    - Recognizing and understanding these biases is the first step toward mitigating their impact. Education about cognitive biases can help investors identify when their decisions might be influenced by irrational thinking.
- **Systematic Decision-Making:**
    - Developing and adhering to a systematic investment process can reduce the influence of biases. This includes setting clear investment criteria, conducting thorough research, and following a disciplined approach to buying and selling assets.
- **Seeking External Perspectives:**

- ◦ Consulting with financial advisors or investment professionals can provide an external perspective, helping to counteract personal biases. Diverse viewpoints can contribute to more balanced and objective decision-making.

In summary, Chapter 4.1 emphasizes the importance of recognizing and mitigating cognitive biases in investment decisions. Understanding these psychological tendencies and adopting strategies to counteract them can lead to more rational, objective, and effective investment choices, better aligned with one's financial goals and risk tolerance.

Understanding Cognitive Biases

Cognitive biases play a significant role in investment decisions, often leading to deviations from rational judgment and optimal decision-making. Understanding these biases is crucial for investors seeking to make informed and effective choices in the financial markets.

Psychological Influences on Decision-Making

- **Inherent Tendencies:**
  - Cognitive biases are deeply ingrained psychological tendencies that can subtly or significantly influence how individuals process information, make judgments, and decide. They often operate below the level of conscious awareness and can distort objective analysis.
- **Impact on Investing:**
  - In the realm of investing, these biases can lead to decisions that are not based on sound financial analysis or that contradict the investor's own strategies and goals. Recognizing and understanding these biases are key to mitigating their impact.

Common Biases in Investing

- **Confirmation Bias:**
  - This bias leads investors to seek out information that confirms their existing beliefs while ignoring or discounting information that contradicts them. It can result in a skewed analysis of investment opportunities, as investors may only consider evidence that supports their preconceived notions.

    - For example, an investor might overvalue a stock because they focus only on positive news about the company and ignore potential red flags.
- **Overconfidence Bias:**
    - Overconfidence bias manifests when investors overestimate their ability to analyze market conditions and predict market movements. This can lead to taking on excessive risks or failing to diversify adequately.
    - An overconfident investor may make more frequent trades or choose high-risk investments without sufficient analysis, believing in their ability to outperform the market.
- **Loss Aversion:**
    - This bias refers to the tendency of investors to fear losses more than they value equivalent gains. It can lead to conservative investment behaviors that are misaligned with an investor's long-term goals.
    - Loss aversion might cause investors to sell off assets too quickly during a market downturn to avoid losses, missing out on potential gains when the market recovers.

In conclusion, cognitive biases significantly influence investment behavior, often in subtle and unconscious ways. By understanding these biases, investors can take steps to counteract them, such as seeking diverse perspectives, relying on systematic decision-making processes, and regularly reviewing their investment strategies. This awareness is crucial for making more balanced, rational, and aligned investment decisions with long-term financial objectives.

Impact on Investment Choices

Cognitive biases can have profound effects on investment decisions, often leading to actions that are misaligned with one's investment goals or strategies. Understanding these impacts is crucial for investors aiming to make rational, objective choices.

Deviation from Goals and Strategy

- **Impact of Emotional Responses:**
  - Cognitive biases often trigger emotional responses that can lead investors to make hasty or ill-considered decisions. For example, in times of market volatility, fear can lead to the premature sale of assets that are performing well, potentially missing out on future gains.
  - Conversely, optimism or attachment to certain investments might result in holding onto assets that are underperforming or depreciating, in the hope of a turnaround that may not materialize.
- **Contradiction with Investment Plans:**
  - Biases can cause investors to stray from their originally laid out investment plans. This deviation can be detrimental, especially if it leads to decisions that are not in line with the investor's risk tolerance, investment horizon, or diversification strategy.

The Endowment Effect

- **Overvaluation of Owned Assets:**
  - The endowment effect is a cognitive bias where investors ascribe more value to assets simply because they own them. This can lead to an irrational preference for these assets, irrespective

of their actual performance or potential.

- **Reluctance to Sell at a Loss:**
    - This bias can make investors reluctant to sell assets that have lost value, driven by the misconception that letting go of these assets equates to accepting defeat or realizing a loss. This reluctance can result in holding onto losing investments for longer than is justified by rational analysis, often to the detriment of the portfolio's overall performance.
- **Implications for Portfolio Management:**
    - The endowment effect can hinder effective portfolio rebalancing and lead to suboptimal asset allocation. It's important for investors to regularly review their portfolios with an objective lens, assessing each asset's role and performance in the context of their overall investment strategy.

In summary, cognitive biases like fear, over-optimism, and the endowment effect can lead investors to make decisions that diverge from their investment goals and strategies. These biases can result in holding onto underperforming assets or selling profitable ones prematurely, impacting the overall health and performance of the investment portfolio. Awareness and understanding of these biases are key to mitigating their impact, enabling investors to make decisions that are more aligned with their financial objectives and strategies.

Mitigating Cognitive Biases

Effectively managing cognitive biases is a critical aspect of successful investing. By recognizing and mitigating the influence of these biases, investors can make more rational and objective decisions that align with their investment goals.

Awareness and Education

- **Recognizing Biases:**
    - The first step in mitigating cognitive biases is to recognize their existence and understand how they can influence decision-making. Awareness allows investors to question their instincts and assumptions, leading to more thoughtful investment choices.
- **Educational Efforts:**
    - Educating oneself about different types of cognitive biases and their potential impacts on investment decisions is crucial. This can involve reading financial literature, attending workshops, or participating in investment forums where these topics are discussed.

Systematic Decision-Making

- **Clear Investment Criteria:**
    - Establishing clear and objective criteria for investment decisions can help in minimizing the influence of biases. This involves defining parameters for selecting, holding, and selling investments based on rational analysis rather than emotional responses.
- **Disciplined Investment Process:**
    - A disciplined approach to investment, which

includes conducting thorough research, analyzing market trends, and regularly reviewing portfolio performance, can counteract impulsive decisions influenced by biases.
    - Systematic decision-making also involves sticking to a predetermined investment strategy, even during periods of market volatility or when facing personal biases.

Seeking External Perspectives

- **Consulting Financial Professionals:**
    - Engaging with financial advisors or investment professionals can provide valuable external perspectives. These experts can offer advice that is devoid of the emotional attachment an individual investor might have, leading to more balanced decisions.
- **Diverse Viewpoints:**
    - Seeking diverse viewpoints, whether from professionals, peers, or through broader market analysis, can help investors see different angles and aspects of investment opportunities, mitigating personal biases.
    - This also involves being open to contrary opinions and being willing to reevaluate one's decisions in light of new information or perspectives.

In conclusion, mitigating cognitive biases in investment decisions involves a combination of self-awareness, continuous education, systematic and disciplined investment processes, and seeking external, objective viewpoints. By adopting these practices, investors can reduce the impact of psychological tendencies on their investment choices, leading to better-aligned decisions with their financial objectives and risk tolerance.

4.2 Emotional Discipline in Investing

Emotional discipline is a crucial component in the realm of investing, where emotional responses can often lead to hasty and ill-advised financial decisions. Understanding the role of emotions and developing strategies to maintain discipline are key to successful investing.

Role of Emotions in Investing

- **Influence on Decision Making:**
  - Emotions, particularly fear and greed, can significantly impact investment decisions. During market highs, greed can drive investors to take on excessive risk, while fear can lead to panic selling in downturns.
  - Emotional responses can often override rational analysis, leading investors to make decisions that may not align with their long-term investment goals or risk tolerance.

Developing Emotional Discipline

- **Maintaining a Strategic Perspective:**
  - Emotional discipline in investing means maintaining focus on long-term goals and not allowing short-term market movements to influence fundamental investment strategies.

    - It involves making decisions based on sound financial analysis and sticking to a predefined investment plan, even during periods of market turbulence or personal uncertainty.
- **Techniques to Foster Discipline:**
    - **Setting Clear Investment Goals:** Establishing clear and achievable investment goals helps in creating a roadmap that guides investment decisions, reducing the likelihood of emotional detours.
    - **Diversifying Portfolios:** Diversification across different asset classes can help mitigate risk and reduce the emotional impact of volatility in any single investment or market.
    - **Regular Review of Investment Strategies:** Periodically reviewing and adjusting investment strategies in response to changing market conditions or personal circumstances can help maintain focus on long-term objectives.
    - **Avoiding Impulsive Reactions:** Developing patience and resisting the urge to make impulsive decisions in response to market news or short-term trends is vital for emotional discipline.

Implementing Emotional Checks

- **Mindfulness and Self-Awareness:** Being mindful of one's emotional state and acknowledging how it may affect decision-making can be a powerful tool in maintaining discipline.
- **Seeking Professional Advice:** Consulting with financial advisors can provide an objective viewpoint, helping to balance emotional responses with rational investment strategies.

In summary, emotional discipline is about controlling the natural emotional responses that arise in the uncertain world of investing. By focusing on long-term goals, diversifying investments, regularly reviewing strategies, and being mindful of emotional influences, investors can make more reasoned and effective decisions. This disciplined approach is essential for navigating the ups and downs of the market while staying aligned with one's financial objectives.

Role of Emotions in Investing

Emotions undeniably play a substantial role in the investment decision-making process. Understanding this influence is crucial for investors aiming to make sound and rational financial choices.

Influence on Decision Making

- **Impact of Fear and Greed:**
    - **Greed:** In periods of market highs or bullish trends, greed can become a dominant emotion among investors. It can drive them to chase performance, often leading to overexposure to risk or investing in assets without proper due diligence. The allure of quick profits or outperforming the market can cloud judgment and lead to decisions that may not be sustainable in the long term.
    - **Fear:** Conversely, during market downturns or periods of high volatility, fear can take over. This may result in panic selling, where investors sell off assets in a rush, often at low prices, to avoid further losses. Fear-driven decisions can lead to missing out on potential recoveries, as investors sell when the market is at or near its bottom.
- **Emotions Overriding Rational Analysis:**
    - Emotional responses, be it excitement in rising markets or panic in falling ones, can overshadow logical and rational analysis. This can cause investors to deviate from their planned investment strategies, leading to actions that are misaligned with their long-term goals and risk profiles.
    - The emotional cycle of investing often leads to buying high (influenced by optimism and greed) and selling low (driven by fear and pessimism), which is contrary to the fundamental principle of

successful investing.

Emotional Bias and Market Cycles

- **Market Cycles Influenced by Collective Emotion:**
    - The collective emotions of investors often drive market cycles. Bull markets can be propelled by widespread optimism and confidence, while bear markets may be deepened by fear and uncertainty.
    - Recognizing these emotional cycles can help investors identify potential overreactions in the market, both positive and negative.

In conclusion, emotions are a powerful and often underappreciated force in investment decision-making. While they are an inherent part of human nature, their impact on financial decisions can be significant. For investors, developing an awareness of how emotions like fear and greed influence their choices, and learning strategies to mitigate these influences, are key steps in aligning investment actions with rational strategies and long-term objectives.

Developing Emotional Discipline in Investing

Emotional discipline is a key component in successful investing. It involves maintaining a strategic focus and adhering to a well-thought-out investment plan, even in the face of market volatility and personal uncertainties. This section explores various techniques to cultivate and maintain emotional discipline.

Maintaining a Strategic Perspective

- **Long-Term Focus:**
    - Emotional discipline in investing is about keeping sight of long-term goals and not getting swayed by short-term market movements. This approach requires a strategic perspective that prioritizes long-term objectives over immediate market reactions.
    - Decision-making should be rooted in sound financial analysis and adherence to an established investment strategy. This helps in avoiding knee-jerk reactions to market fluctuations.

Techniques to Foster Discipline

- **Setting Clear Investment Goals:**
    - Clearly defined investment goals provide a roadmap for making informed decisions. They help in aligning investment choices with individual financial objectives and risk tolerance.
    - These goals also serve as a benchmark against which to measure progress, helping investors stay on track and make adjustments as needed.
- **Diversifying Portfolios:**
    - Diversification across various asset classes is a fundamental strategy for managing risk. It helps

    - in mitigating the impact of volatility in any single investment or market sector.
    - A well-diversified portfolio can absorb shocks better and reduces the emotional stress associated with fluctuations in any specific asset.
- **Regular Review of Investment Strategies:**
    - Regularly reviewing and adjusting investment strategies is essential to ensure they remain aligned with changing market conditions and personal circumstances.
    - This periodic assessment allows investors to make informed adjustments to their portfolio, rather than impulsive changes driven by emotional reactions.
- **Avoiding Impulsive Reactions:**
    - Patience is a virtue in investing. Developing the ability to resist impulsive decisions in response to market news or short-term trends is crucial for maintaining emotional discipline.
    - This involves understanding the difference between reactive and proactive investing and focusing on the latter.

Implementing Emotional Checks

- **Mindfulness and Self-Reflection:**
    - Being mindful of one's emotional state and its influence on decision-making can be a powerful tool. Regular self-reflection helps in recognizing emotional biases and mitigating their impact.
- **Seeking Professional Advice:**
    - Consulting with financial advisors or investment

professionals can provide a more objective perspective. Their expertise can help in balancing emotional biases with rational investment strategies.

In summary, emotional discipline in investing is about maintaining a strategic focus, setting clear goals, diversifying investments, regularly reviewing strategies, and developing patience. These practices help investors make decisions that are rational and aligned with their long-term financial goals, rather than being driven by short-term emotional responses.

Implementing Emotional Checks

Emotional discipline in investing is not just about following a set of rules; it's also about developing a keen awareness of one's emotional state and its influence on decision-making. Implementing emotional checks is a critical step in cultivating this discipline.

Mindfulness and Self-Awareness

- **Recognizing Emotional Influences:**
    - Being mindful involves being aware of one's emotions and how they might be influencing thoughts and decisions. This awareness can be a significant asset in identifying when investment decisions are being driven by emotions rather than rational analysis.
- **Techniques for Mindfulness:**
    - Regular self-assessment and reflection can help investors recognize patterns in their emotional responses to market events.
    - Techniques like journaling investment decisions and the emotions felt at the time can provide insights into how emotions impact decision-making.
    - Practicing mindfulness or meditation can also help in developing a clearer, more focused mindset, reducing the likelihood of emotional decision-making.

Seeking Professional Advice

- **Objective Perspectives:**
    - Consulting with financial advisors or investment professionals can provide an external, objective perspective. These professionals can help in

assessing investment decisions without the emotional attachment that the investor might have.

- **Balancing Emotions and Rationality:**
    - Financial advisors can assist in aligning investment decisions with long-term goals and risk tolerance, helping to navigate around emotional biases.
    - They can also provide reassurance and guidance during market volatility, helping investors stick to their investment strategy and avoid reactive decisions based on fear or greed.

Building Emotional Resilience

- **Educational Resources:**
    - Educating oneself about market dynamics, investment principles, and the psychological aspects of investing can build resilience against emotional decision-making.
- **Support Networks:**
    - Engaging with investment communities or support networks can provide emotional support and diverse perspectives, helping to mitigate the influence of one's own emotions.

In conclusion, implementing emotional checks through mindfulness, self-awareness, and seeking professional advice are key strategies in maintaining emotional discipline in investing. These practices help investors to recognize and manage their emotional responses, leading to more rational and objective investment decisions. Building emotional resilience through education and community support also plays a vital role in sustaining this discipline over the long term.

4.3 Contrarian Investment Strategies

Contrarian investing is a unique approach that deliberately goes against prevailing market trends. This section delves into the rationale behind such strategies and the associated risks, providing insights for investors considering this path.

Contrarian Approach to Investing

- **Defying Market Trends:**
    - Contrarian investors seek opportunities by doing the opposite of the general market sentiment. This often means buying assets that are currently unpopular or undervalued and selling them when they regain favor in the market.
    - This approach is based on the belief that the market consensus can sometimes lead to mispricing of assets, either undervaluing or overvaluing them.

Rationale and Risks

- **Exploiting Market Overreactions:**
    - The core idea of contrarian investing is that markets can be emotional and often overreact to news or events, either positively or negatively. Contrarians believe that these overreactions can create buying or selling opportunities.

    - For instance, a piece of bad news might cause a stock to fall more than is justified by its long-term fundamentals, presenting a buying opportunity for contrarians.
- **Challenges of Contrarian Investing:**
    - **Timing:** One of the biggest challenges in contrarian investing is timing. Predicting when the market will recognize the true value of an undervalued asset is difficult, and contrarian positions may take a significant amount of time to yield profits.
    - **Risk of Misjudging:** Contrarian investing also involves the risk of misjudging market sentiment or the intrinsic value of an asset. What may seem like an overreaction might be a legitimate adjustment to new information.
    - **Patience and Conviction:** This strategy requires a high degree of patience and conviction, as holding a position that goes against prevailing market sentiment can be psychologically challenging.

Implementing Contrarian Strategies

- **Thorough Research:** Successful contrarian investing relies heavily on doing one's own research to understand the true value of an asset, independent of its current market perception.
- **Risk Management:** Given the high risks involved, effective risk management strategies are essential. This might include setting strict stop-loss orders or diversifying across different assets or sectors.

In summary, contrarian investment strategies offer an alternative approach by capitalizing on potential market inefficiencies. While the potential for high returns exists, these strategies require thorough research, a strong understanding of market dynamics, and a considerable tolerance for risk and uncertainty. Contrarian investors must be prepared for the psychological and financial challenges of going against the market grain.

Contrarian Approach to Investing

The contrarian approach to investing represents a distinctive strategy that challenges conventional market wisdom. By opposing the prevailing market sentiment, contrarian investors aim to capitalize on potential market inefficiencies.

Defying Market Trends

- **Going Against the Grain:**
  - Contrarian investors actively look for investment opportunities that are contrary to the popular opinion or trends in the market. This can involve buying assets that are currently out of favor with the majority of investors or seen as undervalued.
  - Conversely, they may also consider selling or avoiding assets that are highly popular or overvalued by market standards.
- **Philosophy of Contrarianism:**
  - The underlying philosophy of this approach is rooted in the belief that the majority opinion in the market can often lead to the mispricing of assets. When the majority of investors are bullish on a particular asset or market, it might become overvalued, and the opposite is true for assets that are broadly bearish.
  - Contrarians seek to exploit these discrepancies between an asset's market price and its intrinsic value, which they believe are caused by the herd behavior of investors.

Key Aspects of Contrarian Investing

- **Identifying Mispriced Assets:**
  - The core of contrarian investing lies in accurately

identifying assets whose market price does not reflect their intrinsic value. This requires in-depth research and analysis to discern genuine opportunities from mere market noise.

- **Psychological Resilience:**
    - Being a contrarian investor often means holding positions that are at odds with the prevailing market sentiment. This requires a high degree of psychological resilience and confidence in one's analytical abilities, as such positions can sometimes take considerable time to prove profitable.
- **Market Timing Challenges:**
    - Contrarian investors face the challenge of timing their investments correctly. While an asset may be undervalued, it might remain so for an extended period before the market corrects its price. Timing these corrections can be challenging and requires patience and a long-term perspective.

In conclusion, the contrarian approach to investing is a strategy that capitalizes on going against prevailing market sentiments. While it offers the potential for significant returns by exploiting market inefficiencies, it requires thorough research, strong conviction, and considerable patience. Contrarian investors must be prepared to withstand periods of potential underperformance and market skepticism before their investment thesis is realized.

Rationale and Risks of Contrarian Investing

Contrarian investing is based on a distinct rationale that often challenges conventional market thinking. However, this approach comes with its own set of risks and challenges that require careful consideration.

Exploiting Market Overreactions

- **Emotional Market Reactions:**
  - Markets are not always rational and can be driven by emotional reactions of investors to news or events. Contrarian investors aim to capitalize on these emotional overreactions—both positive and negative.
- **Identifying Opportunities:**
  - A typical scenario might involve a stock that experiences a significant drop in price following negative news, despite having solid long-term fundamentals. Contrarians see such situations as potential opportunities to buy undervalued assets.

Challenges of Contrarian Investing

- **Timing Challenges:**
  - One of the most significant challenges in contrarian investing is timing. Determining when the market will adjust to reflect the true value of an asset is notoriously difficult. Contrarian positions often require a long-term horizon and may not yield immediate profits.
  - The challenge is compounded by the uncertainty of market dynamics. An asset deemed undervalued may remain so for an extended period, or its price may continue to decline.

- **Risk of Misjudgment:**
    - Contrarian investing involves the risk of misinterpreting market signals or misjudging the intrinsic value of an asset. What might appear as a market overreaction could be a valid response to fundamental changes or new information.
    - There is also the risk of falling into the "value trap" – investing in stocks that are cheap for reasons that are fundamentally detrimental to their long-term growth.
- **Need for Patience and Conviction:**
    - Contrarian strategies require a considerable degree of patience and strong conviction. Holding a position that goes against current market sentiment can be psychologically challenging, especially when facing extended periods of underperformance or criticism from others.
    - This approach demands steadfastness in one's analysis and the resilience to withstand market pressures until the investment thesis comes to fruition.

In summary, contrarian investing offers the potential for significant returns by capitalizing on market overreactions and mispricings. However, it requires a deep understanding of market dynamics, a high tolerance for risk, and the emotional fortitude to withstand market contrarianism. Successful contrarian investors are those who can patiently wait for their analysis to be validated and have the conviction to stick to their strategies despite market skepticism.

Implementing Contrarian Strategies

Adopting a contrarian approach to investing requires more than just a willingness to go against the grain. It demands a disciplined methodology, incorporating thorough research and robust risk management. Let's delve into the key aspects of effectively implementing contrarian strategies.

Thorough Research

- **In-Depth Analysis:**
    - Successful contrarian investing hinges on conducting extensive research to unearth the intrinsic value of an asset. This involves a deep dive into the fundamentals of the asset or company, including financial health, management quality, market position, and growth prospects.
    - Contrarians often look for discrepancies between the current market price of an asset and its intrinsic value as determined by their research.
- **Independent Verification:**
    - It's important for contrarians to rely on their own analysis rather than market sentiment or analyst opinions. This independent verification helps in identifying potential opportunities that the market may have overlooked or misjudged.

Risk Management

- **Managing the Risks:**
    - Given the inherent risks in taking positions that are contrary to market sentiment, effective risk management is critical.
    - This can include setting stop-loss orders to limit potential losses on individual investments. Stop-

loss orders can help in automating sell decisions, removing emotional bias from the exit process.

- **Diversification:**
    - Diversifying investments across different asset classes, sectors, or geographies can help spread and mitigate risk. This is particularly important for contrarian investors, as their positions might sometimes go against broad market movements.
    - Diversification can protect the overall portfolio from significant downturns in any single investment or market segment.
- **Regular Portfolio Review:**
    - Regularly reviewing and reassessing positions is vital to ensure they still align with the initial investment thesis. Market conditions and fundamentals can change, and it's important that contrarian positions are still valid under current circumstances.

Balancing Patience with Responsiveness

- **Patience in Investment Horizon:**
    - Contrarian investing often requires a longer-term investment horizon. Patience is key, as it may take time for the market to recognize and correct mispricings.
- **Responsiveness to Changing Information:**
    - While patience is important, contrarian investors also need to be responsive to new information that might affect the validity of their investment thesis. Being flexible and willing to reassess positions in light of new data is crucial.

In summary, implementing contrarian investment strategies effectively requires a blend of thorough, independent research, stringent risk management practices, and a balanced approach to patience and responsiveness. This approach enables investors to capitalize on market inefficiencies while safeguarding against the inherent risks of going against prevailing market sentiment.

Chapter 5: Global Macro Strategies and Geopolitical Analysis

In an increasingly interconnected world, global macro strategies and geopolitical analysis have become integral to understanding and navigating the complex landscape of international investing. This chapter explores how economic indicators, political risks, and currency markets influence investment strategies.

5.1 Understanding and Capitalizing on Economic Indicators

- **Role of Economic Indicators:**
  - Economic indicators are vital tools for assessing the health and direction of economies. These include metrics like GDP growth rates, inflation, employment data, consumer spending, and manufacturing output.
  - Investors use these indicators to gauge economic trends, policy changes, and potential market movements.
- **Strategies for Utilization:**
  - By analyzing economic indicators, investors can make informed decisions about asset allocation, sectoral investment, and timing market entries and exits.
  - For example, high inflation rates might lead to a shift towards assets that traditionally outperform

during inflationary periods, like commodities or inflation-protected securities.

5.2 Global Political Risks and Their Market Impacts

- **Navigating Political Landscapes:**
  - Global political events, such as elections, policy changes, international trade agreements, or conflicts, can have significant impacts on markets.
  - Political risks can lead to market volatility, affect investor confidence, and influence currency values and commodity prices.
- **Incorporating Geopolitical Analysis:**
  - Geopolitical analysis involves evaluating the stability and policies of countries and assessing how political events or trends could impact investments.
  - Investors might adjust their portfolios to mitigate risks associated with political instability or to capitalize on opportunities arising from favorable political developments.

5.3 Currency Markets and Forex Trading Strategies

- **Currency Market Dynamics:**
  - The foreign exchange (Forex) market is one of the most liquid and dynamic markets, influenced by factors like interest rate differentials, economic data, and geopolitical events.
  - Fluctuations in currency values can significantly impact the returns of international investments and are crucial for investors engaged in cross-border transactions.

- **Forex Trading Strategies:**
    - Forex trading strategies might include carry trades (benefiting from interest rate differentials), hedging against currency risk, or speculating on currency movements based on macroeconomic analysis.
    - Understanding the factors that influence currency values, such as central bank policies and international trade dynamics, is essential for successful forex trading.

In conclusion, Chapter 5 highlights the importance of a global perspective in investment strategy formulation. Understanding and capitalizing on economic indicators, navigating the complexities of global political risks, and mastering the dynamics of currency markets are crucial for investors operating in the global arena. A sophisticated approach to global macro strategies and geopolitical analysis can provide a significant edge in identifying and leveraging opportunities in the international investment landscape.

5.1 Understanding and Capitalizing on Economic Indicators

Economic indicators play a crucial role in shaping investment strategies. They provide valuable insights into the health and trajectory of economies, influencing decisions on where, when, and how to invest.

Role of Economic Indicators

- **Assessment Tools for Economic Health:**
    - Economic indicators are key to evaluating the overall health and direction of economies. They encompass a range of data points, such as:
        - **GDP Growth Rates:** Indicate the overall economic growth and health of a country.
        - **Inflation Rates:** Reflect the rate at which the general level of prices for goods and services is rising.
        - **Employment Data:** Offer insights into the labor market, impacting consumer spending and economic stability.
        - **Consumer Spending:** A measure of the purchasing power and confidence of the general population.
        - **Manufacturing Output:** Indicates the health of the industrial sector and can signal future

economic activity.

- **Predictive Value for Markets:**
    - These indicators are not just snapshots of current economic conditions but can also provide predictive insights into future trends. They help investors anticipate changes in monetary policy, shifts in consumer behavior, and broader economic shifts.

Strategies for Utilization

- **Informed Decision-Making in Investments:**
    - Understanding economic indicators enables investors to make more informed decisions about asset allocation and sectoral investments. For example:
        - A strong GDP growth rate might signal a bullish outlook for equities in that economy.
        - Rising inflation could lead investors to allocate more funds to assets that typically perform well during inflationary periods, such as gold or real estate.
- **Timing Market Entries and Exits:**
    - Economic indicators can guide investors on timing their market entries and exits. For instance:
        - Positive employment data might encourage investments in consumer goods sectors, anticipating increased consumer spending.
        - Conversely, signs of economic slowdown might prompt investors to become more

conservative, shifting towards fixed-income assets or defensive stocks.

- **Sector-Specific Impacts:**
    - Different economic indicators can have varied impacts on different sectors. For example, low-interest rates might be favorable for real estate and construction but less so for the banking sector.

In summary, Chapter 5.1 underscores the importance of economic indicators in crafting investment strategies. These indicators provide crucial insights into economic trends and potential market movements, guiding investors in asset allocation, sector selection, and timing their investment actions. Understanding and effectively interpreting these indicators can offer investors a significant edge in navigating the complex world of investing.

Role of Economic Indicators

Economic indicators serve as vital tools for assessing and understanding the health and direction of economies. They offer valuable insights for investors, policymakers, and analysts alike.

Assessment Tools for Economic Health

- **GDP Growth Rates:**
    - The Gross Domestic Product (GDP) growth rate is a primary indicator of the economic health of a country. It measures the rate of expansion or contraction of an economy and provides insights into its overall performance.
    - A growing GDP indicates a healthy, expanding economy, often leading to increased investor confidence in that market.
- **Inflation Rates:**
    - Inflation rates reflect the rate of increase in prices over a period. They are crucial for understanding the purchasing power of consumers and the cost of doing business.
    - High inflation can erode the value of money and impact investment returns, while low inflation may indicate weak demand or economic stagnation.
- **Employment Data:**
    - Employment figures, such as unemployment rates and job creation statistics, offer insights into the labor market's health. A strong labor market typically indicates robust economic activity and consumer spending potential.
    - High employment rates often correlate with higher consumer spending, boosting various

sectors of the economy.

- **Consumer Spending:**
    - This metric measures the total spending by consumers on goods and services. It's a direct indicator of consumer confidence and a significant driver of economic growth.
    - High consumer spending can signal a healthy economy and is often a positive sign for businesses and investors.
- **Manufacturing Output:**
    - The level of production in the manufacturing sector can indicate the health of the industrial segment of an economy. It can also signal future economic activity and demand trends.
    - Increases in manufacturing output can suggest economic growth, while decreases might indicate a slowing economy.

Predictive Value for Markets

- **Forecasting Economic Trends:**
    - Economic indicators do more than just reflect current conditions; they can also provide forward-looking insights. Investors use these data points to predict future economic activity and market trends.
    - For example, consistent GDP growth might suggest a continuing bullish market, while rising inflation could lead central banks to increase interest rates, impacting various investment assets.
- **Guiding Investment Decisions:**
    - By analyzing these indicators, investors can make

informed predictions about monetary policy shifts, changes in consumer behavior, and overall economic direction.
  - This information is crucial in making strategic investment decisions, such as sector allocation, geographical diversification, and timing market entry or exit.

In conclusion, economic indicators are indispensable tools in the investor's toolkit, providing a comprehensive picture of the economic landscape. Understanding and interpreting these indicators correctly can lead to informed and strategic investment decisions, aligning with broader economic trends and potential future shifts.

Strategies for Utilizing Economic Indicators

Economic indicators are more than just data points; they are critical tools that can guide investors in making strategic decisions. By understanding and effectively utilizing these indicators, investors can enhance their decision-making process in various aspects of investing, from asset allocation to timing market actions.

Informed Decision-Making in Investments

- **Asset Allocation:**
    - Economic indicators can significantly influence decisions regarding asset allocation. For instance:
        - A strong GDP growth rate often indicates a healthy economy, which can be a positive signal for equity investments in that region or country.
        - In periods of rising inflation, investors might shift their focus to assets known to perform well during such times, like commodities (gold) or real estate, as they can act as a hedge against inflation.
- **Sectoral Investment Decisions:**
    - Different economic indicators can affect sectors in various ways. Understanding these nuances can help investors choose sectors likely to outperform.
    - For example, a decrease in interest rates often bodes well for consumer discretionary stocks or the housing market, as consumers have more disposable income and borrowing costs are lower.

Timing Market Entries and Exits

- **Interpreting Economic Cycles:**
    - Economic indicators are valuable in

understanding and anticipating economic cycles. This knowledge can guide investors on when to enter or exit specific markets or sectors.
    - Positive employment trends and increasing consumer spending can signal a growing economy, potentially a good time to invest in stocks. Conversely, weakening economic indicators may suggest it's time to become more defensive in investment choices.

Sector-Specific Impacts

- **Understanding Sector Sensitivities:**
    - Each sector reacts differently to various economic indicators. Recognizing these sensitivities is crucial for sector-specific investment strategies.
    - For instance, low-interest rates generally boost the borrowing-dependent real estate sector but can compress the margins of banks and financial institutions.

Adapting to Economic Changes

- **Dynamic Strategy Adjustments:**
    - It's important for investors to remain adaptable and adjust strategies in response to changing economic conditions as signaled by these indicators.
    - This includes being vigilant about global economic trends and ready to reallocate investments as needed to optimize returns and minimize risks.

In summary, effectively utilizing economic indicators in investment strategies involves a nuanced understanding of how different indicators impact various asset classes and sectors. It requires aligning investment decisions with economic trends and being adaptable to changes in the economic landscape. By doing so, investors can make more informed decisions, better time their market actions, and strategically allocate assets to capitalize on economic shifts.

5.2 Global Political Risks and Their Market Impacts

In the globalized financial landscape, political risks and events can have far-reaching effects on markets and investment portfolios. Understanding and navigating these geopolitical dynamics is crucial for global investors.

Navigating Political Landscapes

- **Impact of Political Events on Markets:**
    - Global political events, ranging from elections and policy changes to international trade agreements and geopolitical conflicts, can significantly influence financial markets.
    - These events can cause shifts in investor confidence, impact market sentiment, and lead to fluctuations in asset prices, including stocks, currencies, and commodities.
- **Volatility and Uncertainty:**
    - Political risks often lead to increased market volatility. Uncertainty about policy outcomes, election results, or international relations can create an environment of speculation, leading to quick and sometimes drastic changes in market prices.
    - For instance, geopolitical tensions or trade

disputes can disrupt global supply chains, affecting the stock prices of companies in the involved countries and sectors.

Incorporating Geopolitical Analysis

- **Assessing Stability and Policies:**
    - Geopolitical analysis involves a thorough evaluation of the political stability and policy directions of different countries. This analysis helps investors understand potential risks and opportunities in various markets.
    - Factors such as government stability, regulatory environment, foreign relations, and social unrest are considered to assess the investment climate of a country.
- **Adjusting Investment Strategies:**
    - Based on geopolitical analysis, investors may adjust their portfolios to either mitigate risks or capitalize on opportunities.
    - In scenarios of political instability or unfavorable policy changes, investors might reduce exposure to affected regions or sectors. Conversely, positive political developments like economic reforms or trade agreements could make certain markets more attractive for investment.
- **Diversification as a Risk Mitigation Tool:**
    - Diversification across different geographical regions and asset classes can be an effective strategy to mitigate political risks. By not over-concentrating investments in one region or sector, investors can reduce the impact of adverse

political events on their portfolios.

- **Staying Informed and Agile:**
    - Staying informed about global political developments and being agile in adjusting investment strategies is key. This involves regularly monitoring international news, analyzing political trends, and being prepared to make swift investment decisions in response to changing political landscapes.

In conclusion, Chapter 5.2 highlights the importance of understanding and navigating global political risks in investment decision-making. Incorporating geopolitical analysis into investment strategies enables investors to identify potential risks and opportunities arising from political events, leading to more informed and resilient investment decisions. In an interconnected world, a keen eye on political developments and an adaptable investment approach are essential for navigating the complexities of global markets.

Navigating Political Landscapes

Understanding the impact of global political events on financial markets is a critical aspect of investing in today's interconnected world. Political landscapes can influence market dynamics in various ways, creating both challenges and opportunities for investors.

Impact of Political Events on Markets

- **Wide-Ranging Influences:**
    - Global political events, including elections, policy shifts, international trade agreements, and geopolitical conflicts, play a significant role in shaping market dynamics.
    - Such events can influence investor confidence, alter market sentiment, and cause fluctuations in various asset classes, including stocks, currencies, and commodities.
- **Economic Implications:**
    - Political decisions can have direct economic implications, such as changes in fiscal policy, regulatory environments, or trade tariffs, which in turn can affect corporate earnings, investment flows, and currency valuations.

Volatility and Uncertainty

- **Market Sensitivity to Political Risks:**
    - Financial markets are often sensitive to political risks, leading to increased volatility. Uncertainty surrounding political events or outcomes can trigger speculative behavior among investors, leading to rapid price movements.
- **Examples of Market Disruptions:**
    - Geopolitical tensions or international trade

disputes can disrupt global supply chains, impacting the performance and stock prices of companies in affected sectors or regions. For example, a trade embargo or sanctions against a country can lead to a sudden increase in commodity prices or affect the stock prices of companies reliant on that market.

- **Sector-Specific Impact:**
    - Political developments can have sector-specific impacts. For instance, defense stocks may react to geopolitical conflicts, while energy stocks might be affected by policies related to climate change or oil production quotas.

Navigating Through Political Changes

- **Staying Informed:**
    - Keeping abreast of global political developments is crucial for investors. This includes understanding the political landscape of countries where investments are held and monitoring upcoming political events that could impact those investments.
- **Risk Management:**
    - Implementing risk management strategies to mitigate the impact of political volatility is essential. This may include diversifying investments across geographies and sectors, or using hedging techniques to protect against adverse market movements.
- **Agility in Decision-Making:**
    - Being agile and responsive to political

developments can help in adjusting investment strategies quickly. This agility enables investors to capitalize on opportunities created by political events or to mitigate risks from potential market downturns.

In summary, navigating the political landscapes requires a keen understanding of how global political events can impact financial markets, leading to volatility and uncertainty. By staying informed, implementing robust risk management strategies, and being agile in decision-making, investors can navigate these complexities and make more informed investment decisions in a politically dynamic world.

Incorporating Geopolitical Analysis

Incorporating geopolitical analysis into investment strategies is essential in today's globalized economy. Understanding the political dynamics of different countries helps in navigating risks and seizing opportunities that arise from political developments.

Assessing Stability and Policies

- **Evaluating Political Stability:**
    - A comprehensive assessment of a country's political stability is crucial. This includes analyzing the strength and stability of governments, the likelihood of political upheaval, and the potential for significant policy shifts.
- **Policy Directions and Regulatory Environment:**
    - Understanding the policy directions of governments and their regulatory environments is important for predicting future economic conditions and market trends. Regulatory changes can significantly impact industries and investment viability.
- **Analyzing Foreign Relations and Social Climate:**
    - The state of a country's foreign relations, including trade policies and international alliances, can have profound effects on its economic prospects. Additionally, the social climate, including factors like labor relations and social unrest, can influence the business environment and market sentiment.

Adjusting Investment Strategies

- **Responsive Portfolio Adjustments:**
    - Geopolitical analysis can inform decisions to adjust

investment portfolios in response to perceived risks or opportunities. For instance:

        - In cases of political instability or unfavorable policy changes, investors might reduce exposure to the affected regions or sectors to mitigate risk.
        - Positive developments, such as economic reforms or beneficial trade agreements, may present attractive investment opportunities, prompting increased investment in those markets.

- **Diversification to Mitigate Risks:**
    - Diversification across various geographical regions and asset classes is a key strategy to reduce the impact of geopolitical risks. By spreading investments, the risk associated with any single political event or decision is reduced.
- **Sector-Specific Considerations:**
    - Certain sectors may be more sensitive to political changes than others. For example, sectors like energy, defense, and finance can be heavily influenced by government policies and international relations.

Staying Informed and Agile

- **Continuous Monitoring and Analysis:**
    - Keeping abreast of global political developments is crucial. This includes regular monitoring of international news, staying updated on political trends, and analyzing how these trends may impact different markets and sectors.

- **Agility in Decision-Making:**
    - The ability to quickly adjust investment strategies in response to changing geopolitical landscapes is a valuable skill. This agility enables investors to capitalize on emerging opportunities and avoid or minimize potential losses from adverse events.

In conclusion, Chapter 5.2 highlights the importance of geopolitical analysis in formulating global investment strategies. Understanding the political stability, policy directions, and foreign relations of countries, and effectively incorporating this analysis into investment decisions, is crucial in managing risks and capitalizing on opportunities in a politically dynamic global market.

5.3 Currency Markets and Forex Trading Strategies

The currency market, also known as the foreign exchange (Forex) market, plays a crucial role in the global financial system. Understanding its dynamics and developing effective trading strategies are key for investors involved in international finance and those looking to benefit from currency market movements.

Currency Market Dynamics

- **Liquid and Dynamic Market:**
    - The Forex market is renowned for its high liquidity and dynamic nature, operating 24 hours a day and involving a wide range of participants, from central banks to individual investors.
- **Influencing Factors:**
    - Currency values are influenced by a variety of factors, including:
        - **Interest Rate Differentials:** Differences in interest rates set by central banks can lead to currency value fluctuations, as investors seek higher returns in different currency markets.
        - **Economic Data:** Indicators like GDP growth, inflation, and employment rates can influence currency strength or weakness.
        - **Geopolitical Events:** Political instability,

economic policies, and global events can cause significant movements in currency markets.

- **Impact on Investments:**
    - Fluctuations in currency values can have a significant impact on the returns of international investments. For investors engaging in cross-border transactions, understanding these dynamics is essential to manage potential risks and enhance returns.

Forex Trading Strategies

- **Carry Trades:**
    - Carry trades involve borrowing in a currency with a low-interest rate and investing in a currency with a higher interest rate. This strategy can yield profits from the interest rate differential, but it also carries risks, particularly from unexpected currency movements.
- **Hedging Against Currency Risk:**
    - Hedging strategies are used to protect against unfavorable currency movements. This might involve using derivatives like currency forwards or options to lock in exchange rates for future transactions.
- **Speculative Trading:**
    - Speculative trading involves betting on currency movements based on macroeconomic analysis. Traders analyze factors like central bank policies, economic data, and global events to predict currency direction.
- **Understanding Central Bank Policies:**

    - Central bank policies, such as changes in interest rates or quantitative easing measures, can significantly influence currency markets. Traders must stay informed about central bank actions and announcements to anticipate market movements.
- **Monitoring International Trade Dynamics:**
    - Trade balances, tariffs, and trade agreements can affect a country's currency value. Traders need to monitor these factors to understand potential impacts on currency markets.

In summary, Chapter 5.3 outlines the importance of understanding the complexities of the Forex market and developing sound trading strategies. Successful Forex trading requires a deep understanding of the factors influencing currency values and the ability to adapt strategies in response to market dynamics. For investors and traders in the Forex market, staying informed, managing risks effectively, and employing a disciplined approach to trading are key to navigating this challenging yet potentially rewarding market.

Currency Market Dynamics

The dynamics of the currency market, or Forex market, play a crucial role in the global financial ecosystem. Understanding these dynamics is essential for anyone engaged in international investing or cross-border financial transactions.

Liquid and Dynamic Market

- **24-Hour Trading and Diverse Participants:**
    - The Forex market operates 24 hours a day, making it one of the most accessible and continuously active financial markets. This around-the-clock trading allows for constant adjustments to global economic events and news.
    - The market encompasses a wide range of participants, including central banks, commercial banks, institutional investors, corporations, governments, and individual traders. Each participant brings different objectives and strategies to the market, contributing to its dynamism.

Influencing Factors

- **Interest Rate Differentials:**
    - Interest rates set by central banks are a primary driver of currency market movements. Currencies from countries with higher interest rates often attract more investors seeking higher returns, which can increase the value of those currencies.
    - Conversely, currencies from countries with lower interest rates may weaken as investors move capital to higher-yielding options.
- **Economic Data:**

- Economic indicators such as GDP growth, inflation rates, and employment statistics significantly influence currency values. Strong economic data can boost a currency's value, while weak data can lead to depreciation.
- For instance, higher inflation can lead to currency devaluation unless countered by rising interest rates.

- **Geopolitical Events:**
  - Political events and geopolitical developments can create volatility in the currency markets. Political instability, elections, changes in government policies, and international conflicts can all lead to sharp movements in currency values.
  - Investors often seek safe-haven currencies like the U.S. dollar, Swiss franc, or Japanese yen during times of geopolitical uncertainty.

Impact on Investments

- **Currency Fluctuations Affecting Returns:**
  - Changes in currency values can significantly impact the returns of international investments. For instance, a strengthening currency can increase the value of foreign investments when converted back to the investor's home currency.
  - Conversely, a weakening currency can erode the returns of foreign investments. This makes currency risk management an essential aspect of international investing.
- **Cross-Border Transaction Considerations:**
  - For businesses and investors engaged in cross-

border transactions, understanding currency market dynamics is vital. Fluctuations in exchange rates can affect import and export competitiveness, profit margins, and overall financial performance.

In summary, the currency market's liquidity and dynamic nature, influenced by interest rate differentials, economic data, and geopolitical events, have a profound impact on global finance and investment. For investors and corporations involved in international markets, a keen understanding of these factors is crucial for effective currency risk management and optimizing the returns on cross-border investments.

Forex Trading Strategies

Successful trading in the foreign exchange (Forex) market requires a comprehensive understanding of market dynamics and the implementation of various trading strategies. These strategies are designed to capitalize on currency fluctuations, manage risk, and leverage economic developments.

Carry Trades

- **Interest Rate Arbitrage:**
    - Carry trades involve capitalizing on the difference in interest rates between two currencies. Traders borrow in a currency with a low-interest rate and invest in a currency with a higher interest rate, profiting from the interest rate differential.
- **Risk Considerations:**
    - While carry trades can be profitable, they come with risks, particularly due to unexpected currency market movements. A sudden devaluation in the invested currency can erase interest gains and lead to losses.

Hedging Against Currency Risk

- **Mitigating Currency Exposure:**
    - Hedging strategies are employed to protect against potential losses caused by unfavorable currency movements. This is particularly important for businesses and investors with international exposure.
- **Using Derivatives for Hedging:**
    - Common hedging instruments include currency forwards and options. These derivatives allow traders to set a fixed exchange rate for future

transactions, providing a shield against currency volatility.

Speculative Trading

- **Betting on Currency Movements:**
  - Speculative trading involves making educated bets on the direction of currency movements. This is often based on macroeconomic analysis, including the assessment of central bank policies, economic indicators, and global events.
- **Analysis of Macroeconomic Factors:**
  - Traders scrutinize central bank policies, such as interest rate decisions and quantitative easing programs, to predict their impact on currency values.
  - Economic data like inflation rates, employment figures, and GDP growth are also critical in gauging currency strength or weakness.

Understanding Central Bank Policies

- **Impact on Currency Values:**
  - Central bank decisions can significantly influence currency markets. Interest rate hikes can lead to currency appreciation, while rate cuts might result in depreciation.
  - Staying updated with central bank announcements and policy shifts is crucial for Forex traders to anticipate and react to market movements.

Monitoring International Trade Dynamics

- **Influence of Trade Policies:**
    - Trade balances, tariffs, and trade agreements can directly affect a country's currency value. A favorable trade balance or beneficial trade agreements can strengthen a currency, while trade deficits or disputes can weaken it.
- **Staying Informed on Trade Developments:**
    - Forex traders need to closely monitor international trade news and developments, as these can offer insights into potential currency market trends.

In summary, Chapter 5.3 outlines various Forex trading strategies, emphasizing the importance of understanding economic indicators, central bank policies, and international trade dynamics. Carry trades, hedging, and speculative trading based on macroeconomic analysis are key strategies employed by Forex traders. Success in this market requires not only a deep understanding of financial and economic principles but also an ability to adapt to the ever-changing global economic landscape.

Chapter 6: Advanced Derivative Strategies

For advanced investors looking to diversify their portfolio and manage risk, derivative strategies offer a range of complex yet potentially rewarding options. This chapter delves into the nuanced world of derivatives, including options, futures, swaps, and structured products, providing insights into their use for both hedging and speculative purposes.

6.1 Options Strategies for the Advanced Investor

- **Options Market Complexity:**
  - Options are versatile financial instruments that give investors the right, but not the obligation, to buy or sell an underlying asset at a predetermined price before a certain date. They can be used for hedging risks or speculating on market movements.
- **Sophisticated Strategies:**
  - Advanced options strategies go beyond basic call and put options, involving combinations like spreads, straddles, strangles, and iron condors. Each strategy has its unique risk/reward profile and is suited to different market conditions and investor outlooks.
- **Risk Management:**

    - Options can be used effectively for risk management, offering protection against market downturns or unexpected movements in asset prices. For example, protective puts can be used to insure a portfolio against significant losses.

6.2 Futures and Swaps: Hedging and Speculation

- **Futures Contracts:**
    - Futures contracts involve an agreement to buy or sell an asset at a predetermined future date and price. They are widely used for hedging risks in commodity markets, currencies, and interest rates.
- **Swaps:**
    - Swaps are derivatives in which two parties exchange financial instruments or cash flows. Common types include interest rate swaps and currency swaps, used to hedge against fluctuations in interest rates and exchange rates, respectively.
- **Speculative Use:**
    - While often used for hedging, futures and swaps can also be employed for speculative purposes. Traders might use these instruments to bet on the direction of market prices or interest rates.

6.3 Structured Products and Their Applications

- **Combining Different Financial Instruments:**
    - Structured products are complex financial instruments created by combining two or more different financial products. These often include a combination of derivatives and other assets like bonds or equities.

- **Customization for Specific Needs:**
    - These products can be tailored to meet specific investment goals or risk profiles. They can offer higher returns, capital protection, or exposure to particular market trends.
- **Diverse Applications:**
    - Structured products can be used for a range of purposes, from generating fixed income to gaining exposure to difficult-to-access asset classes. They are particularly popular among investors seeking customized risk-return profiles.

In summary, Chapter 6 provides an in-depth look at advanced derivative strategies, offering advanced investors tools for sophisticated portfolio management. From leveraging options for hedging and speculation to utilizing futures, swaps, and structured products, these strategies allow for a high degree of customization to align with specific investment objectives and risk tolerances. However, the complexity and inherent risks of these instruments require a deep understanding and careful management.

6.1 Options Strategies for the Advanced Investor

The options market offers advanced investors a platform for sophisticated strategy deployment. These instruments, with their flexibility and complexity, can be tailored for a wide range of investment objectives, from conservative risk management to aggressive market speculation.

Options Market Complexity

- **Versatile Financial Instruments:**
  - Options provide the right, but not the obligation, to buy (call options) or sell (put options) an underlying asset at a predetermined price (strike price) within a specified time frame.
  - Their versatility allows investors to speculate on market movements in either direction or hedge existing positions in their portfolio.

Sophisticated Strategies

- **Beyond Basic Calls and Puts:**
  - Advanced investors often utilize complex strategies that involve combinations of multiple options. These include:
    - **Spreads:** Involving the purchase and sale of two or more options of the same type (calls or puts),

but with different strike prices or expiration dates. Spreads can be bullish, bearish, or neutral.
        - **Straddles and Strangles:** Both strategies involve buying or selling call and put options with the same expiration date. In a straddle, the options have the same strike price, while in a strangle, they have different strike prices.
        - **Iron Condors:** This strategy combines two spreads – a call spread and a put spread – with the goal of profiting from low volatility in the underlying asset.
- **Tailoring to Market Conditions:**
    - Each of these strategies has a unique risk/reward profile and can be tailored to suit different market conditions and investor expectations. Their effectiveness depends on factors like volatility, time to expiration, and the investor's market outlook.

Risk Management

- **Hedging with Options:**
    - Options are powerful tools for risk management. They can be used to hedge against potential losses in an investor's portfolio. For instance:
        - **Protective Puts:** An investor holding a long position in a stock might buy put options to protect against a decline in the stock's price. This strategy acts as an insurance policy, limiting potential losses.
- **Managing Position Risks:**
    - Options can also be used to manage the risks of

other positions. For example, writing covered calls on stocks can generate income while potentially protecting against modest declines in the stock price.

- **Balancing Risk and Reward:**
    - While options can offer significant protection and speculative opportunities, they also come with risks, especially if the market moves in an unexpected direction. Therefore, understanding the nuances of each strategy is crucial for effective risk management.

In summary, Chapter 6.1 provides an insight into the complex world of options trading for the advanced investor. From employing sophisticated strategies like spreads, straddles, and iron condors, to using options for effective risk management, this chapter underscores the versatility of options as a tool for advanced portfolio management. However, the inherent risks and the need for a deep understanding of these instruments highlight the importance of expertise and caution in options trading.

Options Market Complexity

Options are one of the more complex financial instruments available to investors. Their versatility allows for a wide range of strategies that can adapt to various market conditions and investment goals.

Versatile Financial Instruments

- **Rights without Obligation:**
  - Options grant investors the right, but not the obligation, to buy or sell an underlying asset. This characteristic differentiates them from other financial instruments like futures, where there is an obligation to buy or sell.
- **Call and Put Options:**
  - **Call Options:** These give the holder the right to buy an underlying asset at a predetermined price (known as the strike price) within a certain time period. Investors typically buy call options when they anticipate that the asset's price will rise.
  - **Put Options:** Conversely, put options give the holder the right to sell the underlying asset at the strike price within the designated timeframe. These are often purchased when the investor believes the asset's price will fall.
- **Speculation and Hedging:**
  - **Speculation:** Options allow investors to speculate on the future direction of an asset's price with a relatively lower capital outlay compared to owning the asset outright. This can amplify gains, but also losses.
  - **Hedging:** For hedging, options can be used to protect existing investments from adverse price movements. For instance, buying put options as a form of insurance on a stock position protects against a decline in the stock's price.

- **Leverage Factor:**
  - One of the key features of options is leverage. Since options allow control over a larger amount of the underlying asset for a relatively small investment (the cost of the option), they can provide significant leverage. However, this also means that the potential for both gains and losses is amplified.
- **Complexity in Pricing:**
  - The pricing of options is influenced by various factors, including the underlying asset's price, volatility, time until expiration, and interest rates. The complexity of options pricing, often calculated using models like the Black-Scholes model, adds to their sophistication as a financial instrument.

In summary, the complexity of the options market lies in the unique features of options as versatile financial instruments. They offer investors the ability to speculate on market movements and hedge portfolio risks with a level of flexibility and leverage not found in many other types of investments. However, the inherent complexities of options trading, including their pricing and the heightened risks due to leverage, require a thorough understanding and careful strategy.

Sophisticated Options Strategies

For advanced investors, the options market offers a variety of complex strategies that go beyond the basic buying and selling of calls and puts. These sophisticated strategies can be tailored to a range of market conditions and investment objectives.

Beyond Basic Calls and Puts

- **Spreads:**
    - **Definition:** Spreads involve simultaneously buying and selling options of the same type (either calls or puts) with different strike prices or expiration dates.
    - **Types and Market Views:** There are various types of spreads, including vertical spreads (like bull call spreads and bear put spreads), which can be constructed to express bullish, bearish, or neutral market views.
- **Straddles and Strangles:**
    - **Straddles:** This strategy involves buying or selling both a call and a put option with the same strike price and expiration date. It is typically used when an investor expects a significant price movement in the underlying asset but is unsure of the direction.
    - **Strangles:** Similar to straddles, strangles involve buying or selling calls and puts, but with different strike prices. They are often used when an investor expects a significant price movement but wants to reduce the upfront cost of the straddle.
- **Iron Condors:**
    - **Structure:** An iron condor is a more advanced strategy that combines two different spreads – a call spread and a put spread.
    - **Market Outlook:** This strategy is designed to profit from low volatility in the underlying asset. The investor earns a

premium from the options, with the hope that the asset's price will remain within a certain range.

Tailoring to Market Conditions

- **Risk/Reward Profiles:**
    - Each of these advanced strategies has a distinct risk/reward profile, which needs to be understood in the context of the investor's goals and market expectations.
    - The effectiveness of these strategies depends on several factors, including market volatility, the time remaining until the options' expiration, and the investor's outlook on the underlying asset's future price movement.
- **Adapting Strategies:**
    - Advanced options strategies can be adapted to different market conditions. For instance, in a high-volatility market, strategies like straddles might be more favorable, while in a low-volatility scenario, iron condors might be more appropriate.
    - It's important for investors to continuously assess market conditions and adjust their strategies accordingly to optimize their risk and return.

In summary, sophisticated options strategies such as spreads, straddles, strangles, and iron condors offer advanced investors a toolbox for navigating various market conditions. These strategies, each with its unique risk and reward balance, can be tailored to fit different market outlooks and volatility levels. However, their complexity requires a comprehensive understanding of options mechanics and a careful approach to risk management.

Risk Management Using Options

Options are a versatile tool in the arsenal of investors, particularly for managing and mitigating risks. They provide strategic alternatives not only for speculative gains but also for protecting existing investments.

Hedging with Options

- **Protective Puts:**
    - A classic risk management strategy using options is the purchase of protective puts. This involves buying put options for a stock that an investor already holds (long position).
    - The put option acts as an insurance policy, providing the right to sell the stock at a predetermined price, thereby capping potential losses if the stock price plummets.
    - This strategy is particularly useful in uncertain markets or when holding stocks with significant unrealized gains.

Managing Position Risks

- **Writing Covered Calls:**
    - Another common strategy is writing (selling) covered calls on stocks that an investor owns. This involves selling call options for a stock the investor holds, generating premium income.
    - The risk in this strategy is limited to the potential opportunity cost. If the stock's price rises above the strike price of the call, the investor may have to sell the stock at the strike price, potentially missing out on higher profits.
    - However, it offers protection against modest

declines in the stock's price, as the premium income can offset the losses to some extent.

Balancing Risk and Reward

- **Understanding Options Risks:**
    - While options can provide significant opportunities for risk management, they also carry their own risks. The market may move in unexpected directions, and options strategies often involve complex trade-offs between risk and reward.
    - For example, while protective puts can limit downside risk, they also come with the cost of the option premium, which can reduce overall investment returns.
- **Strategic Use in Portfolios:**
    - Options should be used strategically as part of a broader investment portfolio. The key is to align options strategies with the investor's overall risk tolerance, market outlook, and investment objectives.
    - It's also crucial to understand the specific characteristics and risks of each options strategy. This includes factors like time decay in options pricing and the potential for significant losses in some strategies.

In conclusion, options provide a dynamic and flexible way to manage risk in an investment portfolio. Strategies like protective puts and writing covered calls can be effective in hedging against market downturns and managing position risks. However, the use of options requires a thorough understanding of their complexities and risks. Effective risk management with options involves a careful balance between protecting investments and optimizing returns, all while aligning with the investor's overall strategy and risk profile.

6.2 Futures and Swaps: Hedging and Speculation

In the advanced toolkit of financial instruments, futures and swaps play crucial roles in both hedging risks and enabling speculative opportunities. Understanding these derivatives is key for investors looking to navigate complex market dynamics effectively.

Futures Contracts

- **Agreements for Future Transactions:**
    - Futures contracts are agreements to buy or sell an asset at a predetermined price on a specified future date. Unlike options, they carry an obligation to make the transaction.
- **Hedging Applications:**
    - Futures are commonly used to hedge risks in various markets, including commodities, currencies, and interest rates. For instance, a farmer might use futures to lock in a price for their crop, mitigating the risk of price fluctuations by the time of harvest.
    - They are also used by companies to hedge against currency fluctuations in international transactions.
- **Standardization and Market Impact:**
    - Futures contracts are standardized in terms of

quantity and quality of the underlying asset, and they are traded on exchanges. This standardization and exchange-traded nature facilitate liquidity and market transparency.

Swaps

- **Exchange of Financial Instruments or Cash Flows:**
  - Swaps are financial agreements where two parties agree to exchange cash flows or financial instruments. They are typically over-the-counter (OTC) derivatives, meaning they are traded directly between parties rather than on an exchange.
- **Types of Swaps:**
  - **Interest Rate Swaps:** These involve exchanging interest rate payments, commonly fixed-rate for floating-rate payments, and are used to manage interest rate exposure.
  - **Currency Swaps:** These entail swapping principal and interest payments in different currencies, often used by companies to hedge against currency risks in foreign operations.

Speculative Use

- **Leveraging Futures and Swaps for Speculation:**
  - In addition to hedging, futures and swaps are also used for speculative purposes. Traders and investors use these instruments to bet on the future direction of market prices, interest rates, or currency exchange rates.
  - For example, a trader might use commodity futures to speculate on the future price

movements of oil or gold.

- **Risks and Rewards:**
    - While futures and swaps offer opportunities for significant gains, they also come with substantial risks, especially when used for speculation. Market movements can lead to large profits or losses.
    - Understanding the underlying market dynamics and having a clear risk management strategy is essential for anyone engaging in speculative trading with these instruments.

In summary, Chapter 6.2 sheds light on the use of futures and swaps for both hedging risks and speculative trading. These instruments offer versatile solutions for managing financial exposures and capitalizing on market opportunities. However, their complexity and inherent risks necessitate a thorough understanding and a strategic approach to trading and risk management.

Futures Contracts

Futures contracts are a fundamental component of financial markets, offering a range of applications from risk management to speculative trading. Their structured nature and the obligations they entail make them a unique tool for investors and businesses alike.

Agreements for Future Transactions

- **Binding Nature:**
  - A futures contract is a legally binding agreement to buy or sell a particular asset or commodity at a predetermined price at a specified time in the future.
  - Unlike options, which give the holder the right but not the obligation to buy or sell, futures contracts obligate both the buyer and the seller to fulfill the terms of the contract on the specified date.

Hedging Applications

- **Risk Mitigation in Various Markets:**
  - One of the primary uses of futures is to hedge against risks in different markets. By locking in prices for future transactions, parties can protect themselves against price volatility.
  - For example, in the commodities market, a farmer can hedge against the risk of falling crop prices by selling futures contracts. If the market price drops by the time of harvest, the farmer still receives the price agreed upon in the futures contract.
  - Similarly, in currency markets, businesses can use futures to hedge against the risk of currency fluctuations affecting their international

transactions.

Standardization and Market Impact

- **Standardized Contracts:**
  - Futures contracts are standardized in terms of the quantity and quality of the underlying asset. This standardization covers various aspects like the amount of the commodity, quality specifications, and the settlement date.
- **Exchange-Traded Nature:**
  - Futures are traded on organized exchanges, which provides liquidity and transparency to the market. The exchange acts as an intermediary to all transactions, which reduces the credit risk that counterparties in the contract will default.
  - The exchange-traded nature of futures contributes to price discovery and market efficiency, as prices are publicly available and reflect the collective information and expectations of market participants.

In conclusion, futures contracts serve as a critical tool in financial markets, allowing for risk management and speculative opportunities. Their binding nature, standardization, and exchange-traded characteristics make them a reliable and transparent means for various market participants to manage future price uncertainties. Understanding the intricacies of futures is essential for market participants who wish to utilize these instruments for hedging or speculative purposes.

Swaps

Swaps are a type of derivative that can be an effective tool for managing various types of financial risks. They involve the exchange of cash flows or financial instruments between two parties and are primarily used in the over-the-counter (OTC) market.

Exchange of Financial Instruments or Cash Flows

- **Direct Agreements Between Parties:**
  - In a swap agreement, two parties agree to exchange cash flows or financial instruments over a specified period.
  - Unlike futures and options, swaps are not standardized and are not traded on exchanges. They are customized contracts negotiated and traded directly between parties, typically with the assistance of financial institutions.

Types of Swaps

- **Interest Rate Swaps:**
  - **Function:** Interest rate swaps involve exchanging interest payments between two parties. The most common type is an exchange of fixed-rate interest payments for floating-rate payments.
  - **Usage:** These swaps are used to manage exposure to fluctuations in interest rates. For example, a company with a loan at a floating rate might enter into a swap to pay a fixed rate and receive a floating rate, thus hedging against rising interest rates.
  - **Benefits:** Interest rate swaps can help parties manage their debt obligations more effectively, aligning them with their interest rate outlook and risk management strategies.
- **Currency Swaps:**

- **Structure:** Currency swaps involve exchanging principal and interest payments in different currencies between two parties.
- **Purpose:** They are often used by companies and financial institutions to secure cheaper debt by borrowing at the best available rates in any currency and then swapping for the desired currency.
- **Hedging Currency Risk:** Currency swaps are particularly useful for companies operating in multiple countries, allowing them to hedge against currency risks in their foreign operations. By swapping cash flows, they can mitigate the risk of exchange rate fluctuations affecting their profitability.

Swaps are a versatile and powerful financial tool used for risk management and speculative purposes. Their customizability allows them to be tailored to the specific needs and risk profiles of the parties involved. However, their complexity and the fact that they are traded OTC mean they require a high level of sophistication to understand and manage. This makes swaps particularly suitable for institutions and advanced investors who have the expertise to negotiate and manage these intricate financial instruments.

Speculative Use of Futures and Swaps

Futures and swaps, while widely used for hedging, also offer significant opportunities for speculation. Traders and investors leverage these instruments to make bets on the future direction of various market parameters, often with the aim of generating substantial profits.

Leveraging Futures for Speculation

- **Commodity Price Speculation:**
    - Commodity futures are a popular choice for speculation. Traders use these contracts to speculate on the price movements of commodities like oil, gold, agricultural products, and more.
    - By analyzing market trends, global events, supply-demand dynamics, and other factors, traders try to predict whether the price of a commodity will rise or fall in the future. They then take positions in futures contracts accordingly.
- **Financial Futures:**
    - Futures contracts are not limited to commodities; they also include financial instruments like stock indices, bonds, and currencies.
    - Speculators might use stock index futures to bet on the overall movement of the stock market or use currency futures to speculate on forex market fluctuations.

Speculative Use of Swaps

- **Interest Rate and Currency Swaps:**
    - In interest rate swaps, speculators might anticipate changes in interest rate trends and enter into swaps to profit from these expectations.

  - Similarly, currency swaps can be used to speculate on currency exchange rate movements. Traders might enter into these swaps based on their predictions of future changes in currency values due to economic, political, or other macroeconomic factors.

Risk and Reward Dynamics

- **High-Risk, High-Reward Nature:**
  - Speculation using futures and swaps can be high-risk but also high-reward. The leverage inherent in these instruments means that even small market movements can lead to significant profits or losses.
  - It's important for speculators to have a thorough understanding of the markets they are trading in, as well as a robust risk management strategy to mitigate potential losses.
- **Market Analysis and Strategy:**
  - Successful speculation in futures and swaps often requires in-depth market analysis and a well-thought-out trading strategy. This includes staying abreast of market news, understanding economic indicators, and having the ability to quickly adjust positions in response to market changes.

In conclusion, the speculative use of futures and swaps offers traders and investors a way to potentially capitalize on market movements. While these instruments can provide opportunities for significant returns, they also come with substantial risks. Effective speculation in these markets requires a deep understanding of the underlying assets, market conditions, and careful risk management.

As with any high-risk financial activity, it is crucial for participants to approach speculation with caution and informed strategy.

Risks and Rewards in Speculative Trading with Futures and Swaps

The trading of futures and swaps for speculative purposes presents a complex landscape of potential high rewards and significant risks. Understanding the intricacies of these markets and implementing effective risk management strategies are vital for anyone looking to engage in this type of trading.

Understanding the Risks

- **Market Volatility:**
    - The futures and swaps markets can be highly volatile. Prices can fluctuate widely due to a range of factors including economic indicators, geopolitical events, and market sentiment.
    - This volatility can lead to substantial gains for well-positioned trades but can also result in equally significant losses, sometimes rapidly.
- **Leverage Risks:**
    - Futures and swaps often involve leverage, meaning traders can control large positions with a relatively small amount of capital. While this can amplify profits, it also magnifies losses, potentially leading to the loss of more than the initial investment.
- **Complexity of Instruments:**
    - These derivatives are complex financial instruments. Misjudging the market direction, misunderstanding the terms of a contract, or underestimating the impact of external factors can result in substantial losses.

Managing Risks

- **Clear Risk Management Strategy:**

  - Successful speculation in these markets requires a robust risk management strategy. This includes setting clear limits on potential losses, using stop-loss orders, and regularly monitoring positions.
  - Diversifying trading strategies and not over-concentrating on a single market or position can also help manage risk.
- **Continuous Market Analysis:**
  - Traders need to continuously analyze market conditions and adjust their strategies accordingly. This involves staying informed about global economic developments, policy changes, and other factors that could impact the markets.
- **Understanding Contract Specifications:**
  - It's crucial for traders to thoroughly understand the specifications of the futures and swaps they are trading. This includes details like contract size, expiration date, margin requirements, and the underlying asset's characteristics.

Rewards and Opportunities

- **Profit Potential:**
  - For knowledgeable traders who understand the risks, futures and swaps offer opportunities for significant profits. These instruments can be used to capitalize on a wide range of market conditions and views.
- **Access to Diverse Markets:**
  - Futures and swaps provide access to a variety of asset classes and markets, from commodities and currencies to interest rates and indexes, allowing

for a broad range of speculative strategies.

In summary, while futures and swaps offer the potential for substantial rewards in speculative trading, they also carry significant risks. A deep understanding of market dynamics, a solid risk management strategy, and continuous vigilance are essential for anyone engaging in this high-stakes trading arena. The complexity and leveraged nature of these instruments require a careful and informed approach to trading.

6.3 Structured Products and Their Applications

Structured products represent a sophisticated segment of financial markets, offering customized investment solutions that cater to specific investor needs and risk preferences. These products are particularly appealing to investors looking for tailored risk-return profiles or exposure to particular market trends.

Combining Different Financial Instruments

- **Composition of Structured Products:**
  - Structured products are created by combining various financial instruments, typically including derivatives such as options, futures, or swaps, with traditional investment vehicles like bonds or equities.
  - This combination allows for the creation of products with specific payoff structures, designed to meet particular investment objectives or to hedge specific risks.

Customization for Specific Needs

- **Tailoring to Investment Goals:**
  - One of the key attractions of structured products is their ability to be customized. They can be

designed to suit individual investment goals, whether it's capital preservation, income generation, or growth.
    - For example, a structured product might be created to provide a guaranteed return of principal (capital protection) while also offering the potential for upside based on the performance of an underlying asset or index.
- **Risk Profile Alignment:**
    - Structured products can be structured to align with various risk profiles, from conservative to aggressive. They can offer higher returns compared to traditional fixed-income products, albeit often with higher risks.

Diverse Applications

- **Fixed Income Generation:**
    - Certain structured products are designed to provide fixed income, potentially higher than standard bonds or deposit accounts. These can be appealing in low-interest-rate environments.
- **Access to Complex Market Trends:**
    - Structured products can provide exposure to complex market trends or difficult-to-access asset classes. For instance, they might offer exposure to emerging market trends, commodities, or specific industry sectors.
- **Hedging and Speculation:**
    - They can also be used for hedging purposes, protecting against market downturns, or for speculative purposes, leveraging market

movements without direct investment in the underlying assets.

Considerations

- **Complexity and Understanding:**
    - Due to their complexity, a deep understanding of the underlying components and risks is essential before investing in structured products.
    - The performance of these products can be tied to intricate market conditions, and they may include caps, floors, or other specific terms that can affect their risk and return.
- **Liquidity and Costs:**
    - Structured products can sometimes be less liquid than other types of investments, and they may also carry higher fees or costs.

In conclusion, Chapter 6.3 explores the multifaceted world of structured products, highlighting their versatility and customizability. These products can be powerful tools for achieving specific investment objectives and managing risks, but their complexity requires careful consideration and understanding. Investors considering structured products should be aware of their unique features, potential risks, and costs associated with these sophisticated financial instruments.

Combining Different Financial Instruments in Structured Products

Structured products represent a creative and sophisticated segment of financial markets, crafted by blending various financial instruments. They are designed to cater to diverse investment needs and risk appetites, offering tailored solutions that might not be achievable through traditional investment products alone.

Composition of Structured Products

- **Integration of Derivatives and Traditional Investments:**
  - Structured products often combine derivatives like options, futures, or swaps with conventional investment vehicles such as bonds or equities.
  - The inclusion of derivatives allows for the customization of risk and return profiles, enabling the creation of products that can be fine-tuned to an investor's specifications.
- **Creating Specific Payoff Structures:**
  - The combination of different financial instruments in structured products leads to unique payoff structures. These structures can vary widely, from products offering capital protection with potential for upside gain to those providing high-yield opportunities with corresponding risks.
  - For instance, a structured product might be linked to the performance of a stock index, commodity, or basket of assets, offering returns based on the underlying asset's performance while potentially limiting downside risk.

Tailoring to Investment Objectives

- **Meeting Diverse Investment Goals:**
    - Structured products can be engineered to serve specific investment objectives, whether it's for growth, income, or capital preservation.
    - For example, a structured product might offer a guaranteed return of the principal amount (capital protection) if held to maturity, combined with the potential for enhanced returns based on the performance of a linked asset or index.
- **Risk Management and Hedging:**
    - These products can also be used for risk management purposes. Investors might use structured products to hedge against various risks in their portfolios, including market volatility, interest rate changes, or currency fluctuations.
- **Customization and Flexibility:**
    - The flexibility to tailor structured products according to specific risk-reward parameters allows for a high degree of customization. This makes them suitable for investors with specific needs that cannot be met with standard investment products.

In summary, structured products offer a unique way to combine different financial instruments to create customized investment solutions. They allow investors to access a variety of payoff structures and risk profiles, catering to a broad range of investment objectives. However, the complexity and specific nature of these products require a thorough understanding of their underlying components and risks. Investors considering structured products should approach them with a clear understanding of their individual investment goals and risk tolerance levels.

Customization for Specific Needs in Structured Products

Structured products stand out in the financial world for their remarkable adaptability, allowing for customization to meet individual investor needs and risk preferences. This flexibility makes them an attractive option for those seeking tailored investment solutions.

Tailoring to Investment Goals

- **Alignment with Investor Objectives:**
    - Structured products can be specifically designed to align with various investment objectives, providing a level of customization that is not typically available in standard investment products.
    - Whether an investor's primary goal is capital preservation, income generation, or capital growth, structured products can be engineered to match these objectives.
- **Examples of Customized Solutions:**
    - **Capital Preservation:** For investors focused on protecting their principal, structured products can be designed to guarantee the return of the principal amount at maturity, potentially coupled with additional returns if the underlying asset performs well.
    - **Income Generation:** Some structured products might offer regular income streams, similar to bonds, but with different risk-return characteristics.
    - **Growth Potential:** For those seeking growth, structured products can be linked to the performance of equities, indexes, or other assets, providing the potential for higher returns while managing risk exposure.

Risk Profile Alignment

- **Matching Risk Tolerance:**
  - Structured products can be crafted to align with the investor's risk tolerance, ranging from conservative to aggressive profiles.
  - Conservative structures might focus on capital protection and lower-risk income generation, while more aggressive structures may aim for higher growth potential, accepting higher risks.
- **Balancing Risk and Reward:**
  - One of the key aspects of structured products is their ability to balance risk and reward according to investor preferences.
  - For instance, products can be constructed to limit downside risk while still offering a chance to participate in the upside potential of an underlying market or asset class.
- **Diverse Investment Scenarios:**
  - Structured products can be particularly useful in complex or uncertain market environments where traditional investments may not offer the desired combination of risk and return.
  - They allow for the creation of investment scenarios that can cater to specific market views or hedge against particular market risks.

In conclusion, the customization for specific needs is a defining feature of structured products, offering investors the ability to tailor their investment strategies precisely. This customization extends from the definition of risk and return parameters to the alignment with specific investment objectives. However, investors need to have a clear understanding of the product structure, the associated risks, and how these align with their overall investment strategy and risk tolerance. The bespoke nature of structured products makes them a valuable tool for sophisticated investors seeking tailored investment solutions.

Diverse Applications of Structured Products

Structured products offer a wide array of applications, catering to different investment needs and strategies. Their flexibility allows for innovative approaches to income generation, market exposure, and risk management.

Fixed Income Generation

- **Alternative to Traditional Bonds:**
    - Some structured products are tailored to generate fixed income, potentially offering higher yields compared to conventional bonds or deposit accounts.
    - These products can be particularly attractive in low-interest-rate environments where traditional fixed-income investments may not provide satisfactory returns.
- **Income with Potential Additional Benefits:**
    - Structured products designed for income generation might also include additional features, such as potential for capital appreciation or protection features that guard against downside risks.

Access to Complex Market Trends

- **Exposure to Niche Markets:**
    - Structured products can provide investors with exposure to specific market trends or sectors that might be difficult to access through traditional investments.
    - For example, they can be linked to the performance of emerging markets, specific commodities, or niche industry sectors, allowing

investors to tap into unique growth opportunities.

- **Customizable Market Participation:**
    - These products can be structured to offer varying degrees of participation in the underlying market trend, allowing investors to tailor their exposure level according to their risk appetite and investment goals.

Hedging and Speculation

- **Risk Management Tools:**
    - Structured products can be used as hedging tools, helping investors protect their portfolios against potential market downturns or specific risks.
    - For instance, a structured product might be designed to hedge against currency fluctuations, interest rate changes, or declines in a particular market sector.
- **Speculative Opportunities:**
    - In addition to hedging, structured products can also be structured for speculative purposes. They can be used to leverage market movements, offering potentially high returns from changes in the underlying assets or indexes.
    - This speculative use, however, often involves higher risks and requires a thorough understanding of the product and the underlying market dynamics.

In summary, the diverse applications of structured products make them a versatile tool in modern finance. Whether for generating fixed income in low-yield environments, gaining tailored exposure to specific market trends, or for sophisticated risk management and speculative strategies, structured products offer solutions that can be precisely aligned with various investment needs and objectives. However, their complexity and the specific risks associated with each type of structured product necessitate a comprehensive understanding and a careful approach to investment.

Considerations for Investing in Structured Products

While structured products offer a range of benefits and applications, they also come with unique considerations due to their complexity and structure. It is crucial for investors to understand these aspects thoroughly before incorporating structured products into their investment portfolios.

Complexity and Understanding

- **Understanding the Underlying Components:**
    - Investors need to have a deep understanding of the components that make up structured products. This includes knowledge of the underlying assets, the derivatives used (such as options), and how these components interact under different market conditions.
- **Risks and Performance Factors:**
    - The performance of structured products can be highly dependent on intricate market conditions. Investors need to be aware of specific features like caps (which limit the upside potential) or floors (which limit the downside risk), as these can significantly impact the risk and return profile.
- **Need for Expertise:**
    - Due to their complexity, structured products often require a higher level of financial knowledge and expertise to understand fully. Investors may need to consult with financial advisors or do extensive research to grasp how these products will behave in different scenarios.

Liquidity and Costs

- **Liquidity Concerns:**

    - Structured products can be less liquid than more traditional investments like stocks or bonds. This lack of liquidity can make it difficult to sell the product before its maturity, potentially impacting the investor's ability to react to market changes.
- **Associated Fees and Costs:**
    - These products often involve higher fees and costs, partly due to their customized nature and the complexity involved in their creation and management. These costs can include management fees, structuring fees, and costs related to the underlying derivatives.
- **Impact on Net Returns:**
    - The higher costs and potential liquidity issues associated with structured products can impact the net returns for the investor. It's important to consider these factors when evaluating the suitability of these products for individual investment strategies.

In conclusion, while structured products offer customizable solutions and can be an attractive option for specific investment goals, they also present unique challenges in terms of complexity, liquidity, and costs. Investors considering these products should have a thorough understanding of their mechanisms and risks and consider seeking advice from financial professionals. A careful analysis of how these products fit into the overall investment strategy and risk tolerance is essential for making informed investment decisions.

Chapter 7: Ethical Investing and Corporate Governance

In recent years, ethical investing and corporate governance have gained significant importance in the investment world. Investors are increasingly recognizing that responsible business practices can lead to sustainable long-term returns. This chapter delves into the principles of sustainable and responsible investing, examines the impact of corporate governance on investment returns, and discusses the integration of Environmental, Social, and Governance (ESG) criteria in investment analysis.

7.1 Principles of Sustainable and Responsible Investing

- **Defining Sustainable Investing:**
    - Sustainable and responsible investing involves selecting investments based on ethical, social, and environmental criteria, in addition to financial considerations.
    - This approach reflects the belief that responsible business practices are likely to result in long-term profitability and positive societal impact.
- **Strategies and Approaches:**
    - Strategies can include positive screening (investing in companies with positive ESG performance), negative screening (excluding companies involved in harmful activities), and

impact investing (targeting investments with a clear social or environmental impact).

7.2 Impact of Corporate Governance on Investment Returns

- **Corporate Governance and Performance:**
    - Good corporate governance, encompassing factors like management accountability, transparent accounting practices, and fair treatment of shareholders, is increasingly seen as a critical component of a company's long-term success.
    - Studies have shown that strong governance can lead to better investment returns, as it tends to reduce risks and enhance business resilience.
- **Investor Focus on Governance:**
    - Investors are paying more attention to corporate governance practices when evaluating investment opportunities. Companies with poor governance practices may be viewed as higher risk.

7.3 Integrating ESG Criteria in Investment Analysis

- **ESG Analysis in Investing:**
    - Environmental, Social, and Governance (ESG) criteria are becoming integral to investment analysis. ESG integration involves assessing how these non-financial factors can impact a company's performance and risk profile.
    - Environmental criteria look at a company's impact on the earth, social criteria examine how it manages relationships with employees, suppliers, customers, and communities, while governance

deals with a company's leadership, executive pay, audits, internal controls, and shareholder rights.

- **Benefits of ESG Integration:**
    - Integrating ESG criteria can help investors identify companies that are better positioned to navigate environmental and social challenges, potentially leading to stronger and more sustainable returns.
    - ESG-focused investments also align with the growing investor desire to contribute positively to societal and environmental change while achieving financial returns.

In summary, Chapter 7 highlights the growing significance of ethical investing and corporate governance in the investment process. Sustainable and responsible investing, the impact of corporate governance on investment returns, and the integration of ESG criteria represent key considerations for modern investors who are not only concerned with financial returns but also with the broader impact of their investments. As the world increasingly focuses on sustainability and ethical practices, these factors are becoming essential components of investment decision-making.

7.1 Principles of Sustainable and Responsible Investing

Sustainable and responsible investing (SRI) has emerged as a key strategy for investors looking to align their financial goals with ethical and environmental values. This approach goes beyond traditional financial analysis, incorporating ethical, social, and environmental factors into investment decisions.

Defining Sustainable Investing

- **Ethical, Social, and Environmental Focus:**
    - Sustainable investing involves evaluating investments not only on their financial merits but also on their impact on society and the environment.
    - This form of investing is driven by the belief that companies practicing responsible business models are more likely to achieve long-term success and sustainability, benefiting both society and investors.
- **Long-term Viability and Impact:**
    - The underlying principle is that ethical and responsible corporate practices lead to better risk management, more innovation, and ultimately, stronger financial performance in the long run.
    - By prioritizing sustainability, these investment

strategies aim to generate positive societal outcomes alongside financial returns.

Strategies and Approaches

- **Positive Screening:**
  - This approach involves actively seeking out companies that demonstrate positive Environmental, Social, and Governance (ESG) performance.
  - Investors using positive screening look for businesses with sustainable practices, such as environmental stewardship, social responsibility, and ethical governance.
- **Negative Screening:**
  - Negative screening is the process of excluding investments in companies or sectors that engage in activities considered harmful or unethical. This might include businesses involved in fossil fuels, tobacco, weapons, or those with poor labor practices.
  - The goal is to avoid supporting industries or companies that conflict with the investor's ethical values.
- **Impact Investing:**
  - Impact investing specifically targets investments that are expected to generate a measurable, beneficial social or environmental impact alongside a financial return.
  - This can include investing in renewable energy projects, community development initiatives, or companies with a strong focus on creating positive

social change.

In summary, Chapter 7.1 outlines the core principles of sustainable and responsible investing, highlighting its growing importance in the modern financial landscape. This approach emphasizes the integration of ethical, social, and environmental considerations into investment decisions, with strategies that range from positive and negative screening to direct impact investing. As awareness of global challenges grows, sustainable investing is becoming an increasingly crucial aspect of financial planning for investors who seek to make a positive impact while pursuing financial returns.

Defining Sustainable Investing

Sustainable investing represents a paradigm shift in the investment landscape, integrating ethical, social, and environmental considerations into traditional financial analysis. This approach is increasingly recognized not just as a moral imperative but also as a foundation for long-term investment success.

Ethical, Social, and Environmental Focus

- **Holistic Investment Evaluation:**
    - Sustainable investing goes beyond assessing financial performance to include the impact of investments on society and the environment. It involves a comprehensive evaluation of how a company conducts its business, its role in the community, and its environmental stewardship.
- **Responsible Business Practices:**
    - This approach is based on the premise that companies adhering to responsible business practices are more likely to achieve enduring success. It posits that ethical behavior, social responsibility, and environmental sustainability are indicators of a company's overall health and long-term viability.

Long-term Viability and Impact

- **Risk Management and Innovation:**
    - Ethical and responsible corporate practices are often linked to superior risk management and a culture of innovation. Companies that proactively address environmental and social challenges tend to be better positioned to navigate the complex, rapidly changing global landscape.

- **Financial Performance with Societal Benefits:**
    - The goal of sustainable investing is not solely to generate financial returns but also to produce positive outcomes for society and the environment. The idea is that financial success and societal well-being are not mutually exclusive but are, in fact, interconnected.
- **Sustainability as a Driver of Success:**
    - By prioritizing sustainability, investors aim to support and benefit from companies that are not only financially sound but also contribute to the well-being of the planet and its inhabitants. This principle underlines the belief that sustainable business practices are essential for long-term profitability and shareholder value.

In summary, sustainable investing is defined by its comprehensive approach that considers ethical, social, and environmental impacts alongside financial returns. This investment philosophy is grounded in the belief that responsible corporate practices lead to better risk management, innovation, and ultimately, stronger financial performance. By aligning investment choices with these broader considerations, sustainable investing seeks to achieve not just financial gains but also positive societal and environmental impacts.

Strategies and Approaches in Sustainable Investing

Sustainable investing employs various strategies and approaches to align investments with ethical, social, and environmental values. These methodologies enable investors to contribute positively to societal and environmental objectives while pursuing financial returns.

Positive Screening

- **Seeking ESG Leaders:**
    - Positive screening involves identifying and investing in companies that demonstrate strong performance in Environmental, Social, and Governance (ESG) criteria.
    - Investors using this approach look for businesses that are leaders in sustainable practices, which might include efficient environmental operations, robust social responsibility programs, and transparent and ethical governance.
- **Rewarding Responsible Businesses:**
    - This strategy rewards companies with sustainable practices by providing them with investment capital. It operates on the principle that supporting companies with strong ESG credentials can drive market-wide shifts towards sustainability.

Negative Screening

- **Excluding Unethical Investments:**
    - Negative screening is a process where investors deliberately avoid companies or sectors that engage in activities they deem unethical or harmful.

- Common exclusions include companies involved in industries like fossil fuels, tobacco, and weapons, or those with histories of poor labor practices or environmental violations.

- **Aligning Investments with Values:**
  - This approach is about aligning investment portfolios with personal or institutional values. By excluding certain sectors or companies, investors can ensure their investments do not contradict their ethical beliefs.

Impact Investing

- **Targeting Measurable Impact:**
  - Impact investing goes a step further by focusing on investments that are expected to generate specific, beneficial social or environmental impacts, along with financial returns.
  - This approach targets investments that contribute to tangible outcomes, such as reducing carbon emissions, improving education, or enhancing community development.
- **Examples of Impact Investments:**
  - Examples include investing in renewable energy projects to combat climate change, supporting companies that provide affordable housing, or backing enterprises that improve healthcare access in underserved communities.

In summary, sustainable investing strategies like positive screening, negative screening, and impact investing offer investors avenues to align their portfolios with their values. These approaches range from supporting companies with strong ESG practices to avoiding investments in harmful industries and directly targeting investments that create positive social and environmental impacts. As sustainable investing continues to gain traction, these strategies enable investors to contribute to societal and environmental objectives while seeking financial returns.

7.2 Impact of Corporate Governance on Investment Returns

Corporate governance has become a focal point in evaluating the long-term viability and performance of companies. The way a company is governed can significantly impact its financial health, risk profile, and ultimately, the returns it can deliver to investors.

Corporate Governance and Performance

- **Foundation of Long-Term Success:**
    - Good corporate governance is fundamental to a company's sustained success. It encompasses various aspects, including the effectiveness and accountability of management, transparency in financial reporting, and equitable treatment of shareholders.
- **Reducing Risks and Enhancing Resilience:**
    - Companies with strong governance structures are often more adept at managing risks and navigating business challenges. This is because effective governance can lead to better decision-making, more ethical business practices, and greater operational efficiency.
    - Studies have consistently shown a correlation between strong corporate governance and

improved investment returns. Such companies tend to have more reliable and stable growth prospects, making them attractive to long-term investors.

Investor Focus on Governance

- **Evaluating Governance in Investment Decisions:**
    - Investors are increasingly scrutinizing corporate governance as a critical factor in their investment decisions. Good governance practices are seen as indicative of a company's overall health and its ability to create value.
- **Risk Perception and Investment Value:**
    - Companies that exhibit poor governance practices are often perceived as higher risk. Issues like management misconduct, lack of transparency in financial reporting, and unfair treatment of shareholders can raise red flags for investors, potentially leading to undervaluation in the market.
- **Driving Market Trends:**
    - As the investment community places greater emphasis on governance, companies are incentivized to improve their governance practices. This shift is not only reshaping investment strategies but also encouraging broader changes in corporate behavior, aligning business practices more closely with shareholder interests and long-term sustainability.

In summary, Chapter 7.2 highlights the critical impact of corporate governance on investment returns. Good governance is increasingly recognized as integral to a company's risk management, operational efficiency, and long-term financial success. As investors focus more on governance practices, companies are motivated to adopt stronger governance standards, which can lead to better business performance and higher investor returns. This trend underscores the growing importance of corporate governance in investment analysis and decision-making.

Corporate Governance and Performance

The role of corporate governance in the sustained success of companies has become increasingly evident. Effective governance is not just a regulatory requirement; it is a cornerstone of good business practice that can significantly impact a company's performance and investment appeal.

Foundation of Long-Term Success

- **Key Governance Elements:**
    - Strong corporate governance encompasses several crucial elements:
        - **Management Effectiveness and Accountability:** Effective leadership and accountable management are critical for driving a company's strategic direction and ensuring ethical conduct.
        - **Transparency in Financial Reporting:** Transparent and accurate financial reporting builds investor trust and confidence, which is essential for capital markets to function effectively.
        - **Fair Treatment of Shareholders:** Ensuring that all shareholders, including minority ones, are treated fairly and have a voice in critical decisions, is vital for maintaining investor confidence and loyalty.

Reducing Risks and Enhancing Resilience

- **Risk Management and Ethical Practices:**
    - Good governance structures play a pivotal role in risk management. Companies with strong governance are typically better equipped to

identify, assess, and mitigate various types of risks.
    - Ethical business practices, which are part of good governance, minimize the risk of scandals and legal issues that can tarnish a company's reputation and financial standing.
- **Operational Efficiency:**
    - Companies with robust governance are often more operationally efficient. Good governance can streamline decision-making processes, improve corporate accountability, and enhance overall organizational efficiency.
- **Impact on Investment Returns:**
    - Studies and empirical evidence suggest a positive correlation between strong corporate governance and improved investment returns. Investors are increasingly recognizing that companies with sound governance practices are likely to provide more stable and reliable growth in the long term.
    - These companies are often seen as less risky investments, as they tend to be better prepared to handle business uncertainties and market fluctuations.

In conclusion, the importance of corporate governance in shaping a company's long-term success and investment attractiveness cannot be overstated. Good governance is integral to risk management, ethical conduct, operational efficiency, and ultimately, financial performance. As such, it is a critical factor that investors consider when assessing the long-term viability and growth potential of companies. The emphasis on strong corporate governance reflects a broader shift towards more responsible and sustainable business practices in the global marketplace.

Investor Focus on Governance

The emphasis on corporate governance in investment decisions reflects a growing awareness among investors of its critical role in determining a company's long-term value and risk profile. This shift in focus is not just redefining investment strategies but also influencing corporate behaviors and market trends.

Evaluating Governance in Investment Decisions

- **Governance as a Key Investment Criterion:**
    - Investors are increasingly considering corporate governance as an integral part of their investment analysis. Good governance practices, such as strong leadership, ethical conduct, and transparency, are viewed as indicators of a company's overall health and its potential to generate long-term value.
- **Beyond Financial Metrics:**
    - The evaluation goes beyond traditional financial metrics to include how well a company is managed, its ethical practices, and how it addresses issues such as diversity, employee relations, and environmental impact.

Risk Perception and Investment Value

- **Perceived Higher Risk in Poor Governance:**
    - Companies with poor governance practices are often perceived as higher-risk investments. Examples of concerns include management misconduct, opaque financial reporting, and poor shareholder relations.
    - These issues can raise significant red flags for investors, potentially leading to the

undervaluation of a company's stock, as the market might factor in the heightened risk of investing in such companies.

- **Impact on Stock Performance:**
    - Poor governance can lead to scandals, legal issues, and reputational damage, all of which can adversely affect a company's stock performance and investor returns.

Driving Market Trends

- **Incentivizing Better Governance:**
    - The growing investor focus on governance is driving companies to improve their governance structures and practices. This is partly in response to the market rewarding companies with strong governance through better stock performance and lower cost of capital.
- **Influence on Corporate Behavior:**
    - This trend is also encouraging broader changes in corporate behavior. Companies are increasingly aligning their business practices with the interests of shareholders and considering the long-term sustainability of their operations.
- **ESG Integration:**
    - The focus on governance is part of a broader movement towards Environmental, Social, and Governance (ESG) integration in investment analysis. This reflects a holistic approach to evaluating companies based on both their financial and non-financial contributions to society.

In conclusion, the increased investor focus on corporate governance is reshaping the investment landscape. It is driving companies to adopt better governance practices and aligning business operations with sustainable, ethical, and responsible practices. This trend underscores the evolving nature of investment analysis, where non-financial factors like governance are becoming as critical as financial metrics in evaluating a company's worth and investment potential.

7.3 Integrating ESG Criteria in Investment Analysis

The integration of Environmental, Social, and Governance (ESG) criteria into investment analysis marks a significant shift in how investors evaluate companies. ESG factors offer a comprehensive view of a company's practices and policies, impacting its long-term sustainability and performance.

ESG Analysis in Investing

- **Holistic Assessment of Companies:**
  - ESG criteria provide a framework for assessing a company's impact and practices beyond traditional financial analysis. This involves a detailed examination of how a company interacts with the environment, manages social relationships, and governs itself.
- **Components of ESG:**
  - **Environmental Criteria:** This aspect evaluates a company's ecological impact, including its carbon footprint, waste management, and resource utilization.
  - **Social Criteria:** This involves assessing how a company manages relationships with employees, suppliers, customers, and communities. Key factors include labor practices, product responsibility, and community engagement.
  - **Governance:** Governance criteria focus on a company's

leadership, executive remuneration, audits and internal controls, and shareholder rights. This assesses the quality of management, transparency, and accountability.

Benefits of ESG Integration

- **Enhanced Risk Management:**
    - Companies that score well on ESG criteria are often considered better at managing risks, especially those related to environmental and social issues. This can lead to more resilient business models and reduced volatility in investment performance.
- **Alignment with Sustainability Trends:**
    - ESG integration helps investors align their portfolios with broader sustainability trends. Companies with strong ESG practices are often well-positioned to capitalize on opportunities arising from environmental and social trends.
- **Long-term Performance:**
    - There is growing evidence suggesting that companies with strong ESG practices can deliver superior long-term financial performance. This is attributed to efficient resource use, innovative approaches, and improved stakeholder relations.
- **Meeting Investor Expectations:**
    - ESG-focused investments resonate with the growing number of investors who want their investments to reflect their ethical values and contribute to positive societal and environmental outcomes, alongside generating financial returns.

In summary, Chapter 7.3 highlights the growing importance of ESG criteria in investment analysis. Integrating ESG factors offers a more comprehensive approach to evaluating companies, focusing on long-term sustainability and ethical practices. This trend reflects a broader shift in the investment community, with an increasing emphasis on responsible and sustainable investing. ESG integration is not just about ethical alignment but also about recognizing companies that are better positioned to face future challenges and opportunities, potentially leading to better long-term investment outcomes.

ESG Analysis in Investing

Environmental, Social, and Governance (ESG) analysis has become a crucial aspect of contemporary investment strategies, offering a more holistic view of a company's operations and long-term sustainability. This approach transcends traditional financial metrics, focusing on a company's broader impact and practices.

Holistic Assessment of Companies

- **Beyond Financial Metrics:**
  - ESG analysis expands the scope of investment evaluation to include factors that can significantly impact a company's reputation, risk profile, and long-term sustainability.
  - It involves assessing how a company's operations and policies align with environmental stewardship, social responsibility, and ethical governance.

Components of ESG

- **Environmental Criteria:**
  - **Ecological Impact Assessment:** This examines how a company affects the natural environment. Key aspects include its carbon footprint, energy efficiency, pollution, waste management, and the sustainable use of natural resources.
  - **Long-Term Environmental Sustainability:** The focus is on the company's commitment to environmental sustainability, which can include efforts in reducing greenhouse gas emissions, investing in renewable energy, and ensuring sustainable resource usage.
- **Social Criteria:**

- **Management of Stakeholder Relationships:** Social criteria assess a company's relationships with employees, suppliers, customers, and the communities where it operates.
- **Key Considerations:** Important factors include labor practices (such as worker safety and fair wages), supply chain management, customer satisfaction, and community involvement. The emphasis is on creating positive social impact and avoiding social controversies.

- **Governance:**
  - **Corporate Leadership and Ethics:** Governance criteria evaluate the company's leadership, executive pay structures, internal controls, and shareholder rights.
  - **Transparency and Accountability:** This includes assessing the quality and integrity of management, the transparency of financial reporting, and the company's commitment to serving the interests of all stakeholders, not just shareholders.

In conclusion, ESG analysis in investing provides a comprehensive framework for evaluating companies based on their environmental impact, social responsibility, and governance practices. This approach reflects a growing recognition that these non-financial factors can significantly influence a company's risk and return profile. By incorporating ESG criteria into investment decisions, investors can gain deeper insights into the sustainability and ethical practices of the companies they invest in, aligning their portfolios with broader societal values while potentially enhancing long-term investment returns.

Benefits of ESG Integration

The integration of Environmental, Social, and Governance (ESG) criteria into investment strategies is not just a trend but a fundamental shift in how companies and investments are evaluated. This approach offers multiple benefits, ranging from enhanced risk management to alignment with broader sustainability trends.

Enhanced Risk Management

- **Stronger Risk Oversight:**
    - Companies with high ESG scores typically exhibit stronger risk management practices, particularly regarding environmental and social issues. This enhanced oversight can lead to more resilient business models, capable of navigating various challenges and uncertainties.
- **Reduced Volatility:**
    - Firms excelling in ESG often experience less volatility in their investment performance. This stability can be attributed to proactive management of ESG-related risks, which can otherwise lead to reputational damage, legal issues, and financial losses.

Alignment with Sustainability Trends

- **Capturing Market Opportunities:**
    - ESG integration allows investors to position their portfolios to benefit from global sustainability trends. Companies with robust ESG practices are often at the forefront of responding to and capitalizing on these trends, such as the transition to renewable energy or the increasing focus on social responsibility.

- **Future-Proofing Investments:**
    - Investing in companies with strong ESG practices can be seen as an investment in future-proof businesses. These companies are more likely to adapt and thrive in a world where sustainability is increasingly prioritized.

Long-term Performance

- **Financial Outperformance:**
    - There is a growing body of evidence suggesting that companies with solid ESG credentials can deliver superior long-term financial performance. This outperformance is linked to factors like efficient use of resources, innovative business strategies, and strong stakeholder relationships.
- **Sustainable Growth:**
    - Firms that prioritize ESG considerations often foster sustainable business growth, which can translate into steady and reliable returns for investors over the long term.

Meeting Investor Expectations

- **Aligning with Investor Values:**
    - ESG-focused investments are increasingly aligning with investor expectations, particularly among those who seek to make a positive impact. Many investors now view their investments as an extension of their values, opting for companies that contribute positively to societal and environmental objectives.
- **Growth in ESG Investing:**

- The demand for ESG integration in investment portfolios is rising, reflecting a broader shift in investor preferences towards sustainability and responsible business practices.

In summary, ESG integration offers significant benefits, including enhanced risk management, alignment with sustainability trends, potential for long-term financial performance, and the ability to meet evolving investor expectations. As the world increasingly focuses on sustainable and responsible practices, ESG integration is becoming a vital component of thoughtful and future-oriented investment strategies.

Chapter 8: Tax Strategies and Efficient Asset Allocation

In the realm of investment, understanding and implementing effective tax strategies is crucial for maximizing returns. This chapter delves into tax-optimized investment strategies, explores the impact of asset location on tax implications, and discusses estate planning and wealth transfer techniques. These topics are essential for investors seeking to manage their portfolios in a tax-efficient manner while planning for future wealth transfer.

8.1 Tax-Optimized Investment Strategies

- **Minimizing Tax Liabilities:**
    - This section focuses on strategies to minimize tax liabilities on investment returns. It covers various approaches such as tax-loss harvesting, choosing tax-efficient investment vehicles, and timing the realization of capital gains and losses.
- **Utilizing Tax-Advantaged Accounts:**
    - The use of tax-advantaged accounts like IRAs, 401(k)s, or Roth IRAs for retirement savings is explored. These accounts offer different tax benefits that can significantly impact long-term investment growth.

8.2 Asset Location and Tax Implications

- **Strategic Asset Placement:**
    - Asset location involves strategically placing investments in different types of accounts (taxable, tax-deferred, and tax-free) based on their tax efficiency. This section examines how the type of investment (e.g., bonds, stocks, mutual funds) aligns with different account types to optimize tax outcomes.
- **Maximizing After-Tax Returns:**
    - The goal is to maximize after-tax returns by understanding the tax treatment of various investments and using this knowledge to decide where to hold different types of assets.

8.3 Estate Planning and Wealth Transfer Techniques

- **Planning for Wealth Transfer:**
    - This segment addresses the strategies for efficiently transferring wealth to beneficiaries, including considerations for estate taxes, gift taxes, and inheritance taxes.
- **Use of Trusts and Other Vehicles:**
    - The creation and utilization of trusts, wills, and other estate planning tools are discussed. These instruments can be pivotal in managing how wealth is distributed after one's passing while minimizing the tax impact on the estate and beneficiaries.
- **Intergenerational Wealth Planning:**
    - Strategies for intergenerational wealth transfer are explored, including gifting, charitable donations, and the strategic use of life insurance policies.

In summary, Chapter 8 provides a comprehensive guide on how to approach investment and estate planning with a keen eye on tax implications. From optimizing investment strategies for tax efficiency to strategic asset location and estate planning, this chapter offers valuable insights for investors looking to preserve and grow their wealth while minimizing tax liabilities. The integration of these strategies can play a crucial role in effective financial planning and wealth management.

8.1 Tax-Optimized Investment Strategies

Tax optimization is a critical aspect of investment strategy, directly impacting the net returns on investments. This section delves into various methods by which investors can minimize their tax liabilities and enhance their investment efficiency.

Minimizing Tax Liabilities

- **Tax-Loss Harvesting:**
  - Tax-loss harvesting involves selling securities at a loss to offset capital gains tax liabilities. This strategy can be particularly effective in managing the tax impact of investment gains.
  - It requires careful monitoring of the investment portfolio to identify opportunities where realizing a loss can be advantageous from a tax perspective.
- **Tax-Efficient Investment Vehicles:**
  - Choosing investment vehicles that are tax-efficient can significantly reduce the tax burden. This includes investments like index funds or ETFs, which typically have lower turnover and thus lower capital gains distributions.
  - Understanding the tax implications of different types of investment vehicles (e.g., mutual funds, stocks, bonds) is key to selecting the right mix to

minimize tax exposure.

- **Timing of Capital Gains and Losses:**
    - The timing of realizing capital gains and losses can impact tax liabilities. Investors can strategically plan the sale of assets to manage their tax bracket effectively.
    - Long-term capital gains are typically taxed at a lower rate than short-term gains, making it beneficial to hold investments for longer periods.

Utilizing Tax-Advantaged Accounts

- **Retirement Accounts:**
    - Tax-advantaged accounts such as Individual Retirement Accounts (IRAs), 401(k)s, and Roth IRAs are essential tools for retirement savings. Each of these accounts has unique tax implications:
        - **Traditional IRAs and 401(k)s:** Contributions are often tax-deductible, but withdrawals are taxed as ordinary income.
        - **Roth IRAs:** Contributions are made with after-tax dollars, but withdrawals during retirement are tax-free.
- **Maximizing Long-Term Growth:**
    - Utilizing these tax-advantaged accounts can significantly enhance long-term investment growth. The tax-deferred or tax-free growth allows investments to compound more efficiently over time.
- **Strategic Contributions and Withdrawals:**
    - Making strategic contributions to and withdrawals from these accounts can optimize tax

benefits. This includes considering factors such as current tax rates, expected future tax rates, and required minimum distributions.

In summary, Chapter 8.1 outlines strategies for tax-optimized investing, emphasizing the importance of understanding and utilizing tax-loss harvesting, tax-efficient investment vehicles, and tax-advantaged retirement accounts. By implementing these strategies, investors can effectively reduce their tax liabilities and enhance the growth potential of their investments. Proper tax planning is integral to maximizing the net returns on investments and achieving long-term financial goals.

Minimizing Tax Liabilities

Effectively managing tax liabilities is a critical aspect of maximizing investment returns. This section outlines strategies like tax-loss harvesting, selecting tax-efficient investment vehicles, and the strategic timing of realizing capital gains and losses.

Tax-Loss Harvesting

- **Offsetting Gains with Losses:**
  - Tax-loss harvesting is a strategy where investors sell securities at a loss to offset capital gains taxes on other investments. This can be a practical approach to reduce the overall tax burden.
- **Portfolio Monitoring:**
  - Implementing this strategy requires diligent monitoring of the investment portfolio to identify situations where selling a security at a loss is advantageous from a tax standpoint.
- **Considerations and Constraints:**
  - It's important to consider the 'wash-sale' rule, which prohibits claiming a loss on a security if a substantially identical security is purchased within 30 days before or after the sale.

Tax-Efficient Investment Vehicles

- **Choosing Low Turnover Investments:**
  - Opting for tax-efficient investment vehicles like index funds or Exchange-Traded Funds (ETFs) can help minimize tax liabilities. These vehicles typically have lower turnover rates, resulting in fewer capital gains distributions.
- **Assessing Tax Implications:**

    - Understanding the tax implications of various investment vehicles is crucial. For example, mutual funds may generate capital gains distributions, whereas stocks and bonds have different tax treatments based on dividends and interest income.

Timing of Capital Gains and Losses

- **Strategic Realization of Gains:**
    - The timing of when to realize capital gains and losses can significantly affect tax liabilities. Investors can strategically plan the sale of assets to align with their current tax bracket and future tax expectations.
- **Benefit of Long-Term Holdings:**
    - Long-term capital gains, which apply to investments held for more than a year, are typically taxed at a lower rate than short-term gains. Therefore, holding investments for longer periods can be tax advantageous.

In summary, minimizing tax liabilities through strategies like tax-loss harvesting, selecting tax-efficient investment vehicles, and the strategic timing of capital gains and losses is an integral part of sophisticated investment management. These approaches require a deep understanding of tax laws and careful planning to optimize the tax efficiency of an investment portfolio. By effectively implementing these strategies, investors can significantly reduce their tax burden and enhance the overall performance of their investments.

Utilizing Tax-Advantaged Accounts

Tax-advantaged accounts play a crucial role in retirement planning, offering significant benefits that can enhance long-term financial growth. Understanding the unique features of these accounts is key to maximizing their advantages.

Retirement Accounts

- **Traditional IRAs and 401(k)s:**
  - **Tax-Deductible Contributions:** Contributions to Traditional IRAs and 401(k)s can often be deducted from taxable income, providing an immediate tax benefit.
  - **Taxation on Withdrawals:** Withdrawals from these accounts are taxed as ordinary income. Since many individuals are in a lower tax bracket during retirement, this can lead to tax savings.
  - **Deferred Taxation:** The deferral of taxes on investment gains allows the investments within these accounts to grow tax-free until withdrawal.
- **Roth IRAs:**
  - **After-Tax Contributions:** Contributions to Roth IRAs are made with after-tax dollars, meaning there's no tax deduction at the time of contribution.
  - **Tax-Free Withdrawals:** Withdrawals from a Roth IRA during retirement are tax-free, including the earnings. This can be particularly advantageous for those who expect to be in a higher tax bracket during retirement.
  - **No Required Minimum Distributions (RMDs):** Unlike Traditional IRAs, Roth IRAs do not have required minimum distributions, allowing for more flexible estate planning.

Maximizing Long-Term Growth

- **Compounding Benefits:**
    - The tax-deferred or tax-free nature of these accounts allows investments to compound over time without the drag of taxes. This can significantly enhance the growth potential of retirement savings.
- **Long-Term Strategy:**
    - By taking advantage of the tax benefits and compounding interest, these accounts can play a vital role in achieving long-term financial goals, particularly retirement readiness.

Strategic Contributions and Withdrawals

- **Planning Contributions:**
    - Deciding between Traditional and Roth accounts often depends on current and expected future tax rates. If you expect to be in a higher tax bracket in retirement, Roth accounts may be more advantageous.
- **Withdrawal Strategies:**
    - Developing a strategy for withdrawals is crucial, especially for accounts with RMDs. Timing withdrawals to minimize tax liabilities can involve a combination of taking distributions from both Roth and Traditional accounts.

In conclusion, Chapter 8.1 emphasizes the importance of utilizing tax-advantaged retirement accounts as a cornerstone of effective financial planning. Understanding the differences between Traditional IRAs, 401(k)s, and Roth IRAs, and strategically planning contributions and withdrawals, can significantly impact the growth and accessibility of retirement savings. These accounts offer unique benefits that, when leveraged correctly, can provide substantial advantages in pursuit of long-term financial goals.

8.2 Asset Location and Tax Implications

Asset location is a strategic approach to investment that considers the tax implications of different types of accounts and the characteristics of various investments. Proper asset location can significantly enhance the after-tax return of an investment portfolio.

Strategic Asset Placement

- **Aligning Investments with Account Types:**
    - Asset location is about placing investments in the most tax-efficient accounts. This involves understanding how different investments are taxed and choosing the right type of account (taxable, tax-deferred, or tax-free) for each investment.
    - For example, high-yield bonds might be best placed in tax-deferred accounts like a traditional IRA, where the interest income won't be taxed until withdrawal, while stocks held for the long term may be better suited for taxable accounts due to favorable capital gains tax rates.
- **Considerations for Different Investments:**
    - The strategy takes into account the tax treatment of various investment types:
        - **Interest-Earning Investments:** These are often

best placed in tax-deferred accounts to avoid higher taxes on interest income.

- **Capital Appreciation Investments:** Stocks and mutual funds that primarily offer capital appreciation might be more tax-efficient in taxable accounts, where long-term capital gains are taxed at lower rates.
- **Dividend-Paying Investments:** The placement of dividend-paying stocks depends on the nature of the dividends (qualified or non-qualified) and the investor's tax bracket.

Maximizing After-Tax Returns

- **Understanding Tax Treatment:**
  - A deep understanding of the tax treatment of different investment types is crucial. This includes knowing the tax rates for capital gains, dividends, and interest income, as well as understanding how these rates apply to different account types.
- **Holistic Portfolio Approach:**
  - Asset location should be considered as part of a holistic investment strategy. It involves not only the selection of securities but also deciding where to place these securities to optimize tax efficiency.
- **Long-Term Perspective:**
  - The focus is on maximizing long-term, after-tax returns. This might mean sacrificing some short-term efficiency for a greater long-term benefit.
- **Periodic Review and Adjustment:**
  - Tax laws and personal circumstances can change, so it's important to review and adjust the asset

location strategy periodically to maintain its tax efficiency.

In conclusion, Chapter 8.2 highlights the importance of asset location in investment strategy. By strategically placing assets in the most tax-efficient accounts, investors can significantly enhance the after-tax returns of their portfolios. This approach requires an understanding of both the tax treatment of various types of investments and the characteristics of different account types. Effective asset location is a dynamic process and should be regularly reviewed to adapt to changes in tax laws and personal financial situations.

Strategic Asset Placement

Strategic asset placement focuses on optimizing the tax efficiency of an investment portfolio by aligning different types of investments with the most suitable account types. This strategy is crucial for enhancing after-tax returns and overall investment performance.

Aligning Investments with Account Types

- **Tax-Efficient Allocation:**
    - The key to effective asset location is understanding the differing tax treatments of various accounts and aligning investments accordingly.
    - **Example:** High-yield bonds, which generate regular interest income typically taxed at ordinary income rates, can be ideally placed in tax-deferred accounts like Traditional IRAs. Here, the tax on interest income is deferred until withdrawal, potentially at a lower tax rate in retirement.
    - Conversely, stocks aimed at long-term capital appreciation may be better suited for taxable accounts due to lower long-term capital gains tax rates.

Considerations for Different Investments

- **Interest-Earning Investments:**
    - Placing interest-earning securities like bonds and CDs in tax-deferred accounts can shield investors from higher immediate tax liabilities on interest income.
- **Capital Appreciation Investments:**
    - Stocks and mutual funds that are expected to appreciate over time are often more tax-efficient in

taxable accounts. The tax benefit arises from the lower long-term capital gains rates applicable to investments held for more than a year.

- **Dividend-Paying Investments:**
    - The optimal location for dividend-paying stocks depends on the nature of the dividends and the investor's tax situation.
        - **Qualified Dividends:** Often taxed at a lower rate, similar to long-term capital gains, which might make them suitable for taxable accounts.
        - **Non-Qualified Dividends:** These are taxed as ordinary income and might be better placed in tax-deferred accounts.

In summary, Chapter 8.2 underscores the importance of strategic asset placement in tax-efficient investing. By carefully aligning various types of investments with the most appropriate account types—taxable, tax-deferred, or tax-free—investors can significantly enhance the after-tax performance of their portfolios. This strategy requires a thorough understanding of both the tax characteristics of different investments and the tax rules governing different types of accounts. Regular review and adjustment of this strategy are essential to adapt to changes in tax laws and individual financial circumstances.

Maximizing After-Tax Returns

Effectively maximizing after-tax returns is a cornerstone of successful investing. It requires a nuanced understanding of tax treatments and a comprehensive approach to portfolio management, ensuring that investments are not only profitable but also tax-efficient.

Understanding Tax Treatment

- **Knowledge of Tax Rates and Implications:**

    - Investors must be well-versed in the tax rates applicable to different types of investment income, including capital gains, dividends, and interest.
    - Understanding how these rates vary based on the holding period (short-term vs. long-term) and the type of investment account (taxable, tax-deferred, tax-free) is crucial.
- **Applying Tax Knowledge to Investment Decisions:**
    - This knowledge allows investors to make informed decisions about which investments to place in which accounts to minimize the tax burden. For instance, knowing that long-term capital gains are taxed more favorably than short-term gains can influence decisions on buying and selling assets.

Holistic Portfolio Approach

- **Integrating Tax Strategy with Investment Selection:**
    - Asset location should be an integral part of the overall investment strategy, considering both the potential returns of investments and their tax implications.
    - This approach involves strategically placing assets across various account types to create a balanced, diversified portfolio that is tax-efficient.

Long-Term Perspective

- **Focusing on Long-Term Gains:**
    - The primary goal is to maximize long-term, after-tax returns. This perspective may involve making

decisions that are less tax-efficient in the short term but offer greater tax benefits over the long haul.
    - For example, holding investments longer to qualify for long-term capital gains tax rates, even if it means paying taxes on dividends in the interim.

Periodic Review and Adjustment

- **Adapting to Changes:**
    - Tax laws and personal financial circumstances are not static; they can change over time. Therefore, it's important to periodically review and adjust the asset location strategy to ensure continued tax efficiency.
    - Changes in income, tax laws, or financial goals can all warrant a reassessment of how assets are allocated across different accounts.

In conclusion, maximizing after-tax returns requires a strategic approach that encompasses a deep understanding of tax treatments, a holistic view of portfolio management, and a long-term perspective. Regular review and adaptation of this strategy are also essential to respond to evolving tax laws and personal financial situations. By employing these practices, investors can significantly enhance the effectiveness and efficiency of their investment strategies, leading to greater financial success over the long term.

8.3 Estate Planning and Wealth Transfer Techniques

Estate planning and wealth transfer are critical components of financial planning, particularly for individuals looking to preserve their wealth and ensure its efficient transfer to future generations. This chapter delves into various strategies and tools designed to facilitate the transfer of wealth in a tax-efficient manner, while also fulfilling the individual's personal and family objectives.

Planning for Wealth Transfer

- **Navigating Taxes and Regulations:**
    - Effective wealth transfer planning involves understanding and navigating complex estate, gift, and inheritance tax laws. This includes knowing tax thresholds, exemptions, and the most tax-efficient methods of transferring wealth.
    - Strategies need to be tailored to individual circumstances, considering the size of the estate, the number of beneficiaries, and specific family dynamics.
- **Holistic Approach to Wealth Transfer:**
    - A comprehensive wealth transfer plan encompasses more than just financial assets. It also includes considerations for real estate, business interests, and personal items of value or

sentimental significance.

Use of Trusts and Other Vehicles

- **Trusts as Flexible Tools:**
    - Trusts are versatile estate planning tools that can provide control over how and when assets are distributed. Different types of trusts, such as living trusts, irrevocable trusts, and charitable trusts, serve various purposes and offer different benefits and limitations.
    - Trusts can help minimize estate taxes, protect assets from creditors, and ensure that wealth is used according to the grantor's wishes.
- **Wills and Other Legal Instruments:**
    - Wills are fundamental in estate planning, dictating the distribution of assets and the care of any minor children. Other tools like powers of attorney and healthcare directives are also important for comprehensive planning.

Intergenerational Wealth Planning

- **Gifting Strategies:**
    - Implementing a gifting strategy can be an effective way to transfer wealth. This might involve taking advantage of annual gift tax exclusions or making direct payments for medical or educational expenses, which are often exempt from gift taxes.
- **Charitable Contributions:**
    - Charitable giving can be part of an estate plan, providing tax benefits while fulfilling philanthropic goals. Strategies might include

charitable trusts or donor-advised funds.

- **Life Insurance for Wealth Preservation:**
    - Life insurance policies can be strategically used in estate planning. They can provide liquidity to pay estate taxes, equalize inheritances among beneficiaries, or simply ensure that there's a financial legacy left behind.

In conclusion, Chapter 8.3 provides valuable insights into the complexities of estate planning and wealth transfer. It emphasizes the importance of using a variety of tools and strategies to ensure that wealth is transferred efficiently and in accordance with the individual's wishes. Effective estate planning is essential for minimizing tax liabilities, protecting assets, and maintaining family harmony during the wealth transfer process. Regular updates and reviews of the estate plan are crucial to adapt to changes in laws, family circumstances, and personal preferences.

Planning for Wealth Transfer

Effective wealth transfer planning is a critical aspect of estate management. It involves a deep understanding of tax implications and a comprehensive approach to ensure that wealth is distributed according to the individual's wishes, in the most tax-efficient manner.

Navigating Taxes and Regulations

- **Understanding Tax Implications:**
    - A crucial part of wealth transfer planning is understanding the intricacies of estate, gift, and inheritance taxes. Knowledge of tax thresholds and exemptions is essential to minimize the tax burden on the estate and beneficiaries.
    - This includes being aware of federal and state tax laws, which can vary significantly and impact the overall tax strategy.
- **Tailoring Strategies:**
    - Wealth transfer strategies should be customized based on individual circumstances. This involves considering the size and complexity of the estate, the number of beneficiaries, and their specific needs or circumstances.
    - It's important to account for potential changes in tax laws and regulations, adapting the strategy as needed to maintain its effectiveness.

Holistic Approach to Wealth Transfer

- **Beyond Financial Assets:**
    - Comprehensive wealth transfer planning extends beyond mere financial assets. It encompasses real estate, family businesses, investments, personal belongings, and even items of sentimental value.

    - Each asset type may have different implications for transfer and taxation, necessitating a diverse set of strategies to handle each effectively.
- **Incorporating Non-Financial Considerations:**
    - The plan should also address non-financial aspects, such as the care of dependents, guardianship decisions, and philanthropic aspirations.
    - Ensuring that personal wishes are respected and that assets are used in a manner consistent with the individual's values and goals is an integral part of the planning process.

In conclusion, planning for wealth transfer is a complex but essential task that goes beyond tax considerations. It requires a tailored approach, considering both the financial and personal aspects of an estate. A well-structured plan not only seeks to minimize tax liabilities but also ensures that wealth is transferred smoothly and in accordance with the individual's wishes, taking into account the unique dynamics of each family. Regular review and adaptation of the plan are necessary to navigate changes in laws, family circumstances, and personal preferences.

Use of Trusts and Other Vehicles in Estate Planning

Trusts and other legal instruments are integral components of comprehensive estate planning. They offer flexibility and control in managing and distributing an individual's assets, providing both financial and personal benefits.

Trusts as Flexible Tools

- **Versatility of Trusts:**
    - Trusts are highly versatile tools in estate planning, allowing for a wide range of structures tailored to

specific needs and goals.

    - **Living Trusts:** These are created during the grantor's lifetime and can be altered or revoked. They are useful for managing assets during the grantor's life and can facilitate the transfer of assets upon death, often bypassing the probate process.
    - **Irrevocable Trusts:** Once established, these cannot be easily altered or revoked. They offer tax benefits and asset protection but at the cost of control over the assets.
    - **Charitable Trusts:** These are designed to provide a benefit to a charitable organization while offering tax benefits to the grantor.
- **Benefits of Trusts:**
    - **Minimizing Estate Taxes:** Trusts can be structured to reduce the taxable estate, potentially resulting in significant tax savings.
    - **Asset Protection:** Trusts can provide protection against creditors, lawsuits, or other claims, safeguarding the assets for the intended beneficiaries.
    - **Control Over Distribution:** Trusts allow the grantor to specify how and when assets are distributed, ensuring that the assets are used according to their wishes.

Wills and Other Legal Instruments

- **Importance of Wills:**
    - Wills are fundamental in estate planning, detailing how assets should be distributed after death. They are critical for appointing guardians for minor children and can be used in conjunction with trusts for a more comprehensive estate plan.

- **Additional Legal Tools:**
  - **Powers of Attorney:** These documents authorize another person to make financial or healthcare decisions on behalf of the grantor if they become incapacitated.
  - **Healthcare Directives:** Also known as living wills, these outline the grantor's wishes regarding medical treatment in situations where they can no longer express informed consent.
  - **Beneficiary Designations:** Updating beneficiary designations on accounts like life insurance and retirement plans is crucial, as these often supersede instructions in wills.

In summary, trusts, wills, and other legal instruments are key to effective estate planning. They provide mechanisms to control asset distribution, protect wealth, and ensure that an individual's wishes are fulfilled. Each tool offers unique benefits and should be selected and structured based on individual circumstances, goals, and legal requirements. Regular review and updating of these instruments are essential to reflect changes in life circumstances, financial situations, and laws.

Intergenerational Wealth Planning

Intergenerational wealth planning is a critical aspect of estate planning, focused on efficiently transferring wealth across generations. This process involves various strategies, including gifting, charitable contributions, and the use of life insurance, all aimed at preserving wealth and fulfilling the long-term financial goals of a family.

Gifting Strategies

- **Leveraging Gift Tax Exclusions:**
  - One common strategy is to utilize the annual gift tax exclusion, which allows an individual to give a certain amount to others each year without incurring gift tax.
  - This approach can effectively reduce the size of an estate over time, thereby potentially lowering estate taxes upon the individual's passing.
- **Direct Payments for Expenses:**
  - Making direct payments for specific expenses, such as medical bills or educational costs, can also be an efficient way to transfer wealth. These payments are often exempt from gift taxes, making them a favorable option for financial assistance to family members.

Charitable Contributions

- **Incorporating Philanthropy:**
  - Charitable giving can be a meaningful component of an estate plan. It not only serves philanthropic interests but can also provide significant tax benefits.
- **Use of Charitable Trusts and Donor-Advised Funds:**

    - Strategies like establishing charitable trusts or donor-advised funds allow for a structured approach to philanthropy. These vehicles can offer ongoing tax advantages and enable the grantor to have a lasting impact on causes they care about.

Life Insurance for Wealth Preservation

- **Estate Liquidity and Tax Planning:**
    - Life insurance policies can be a powerful tool in estate planning. They can provide liquidity to the estate for paying taxes and other expenses, ensuring that other assets do not need to be liquidated under unfavorable conditions.
- **Equalizing Inheritances:**
    - In situations where assets are unevenly distributed, life insurance can be used to equalize inheritances among beneficiaries. This is particularly useful in families with complex asset distributions or business interests.
- **Legacy Creation:**
    - Life insurance can also be used to create or enhance a financial legacy, providing a guaranteed sum to beneficiaries that can be significantly greater than the premiums paid.

In conclusion, intergenerational wealth planning involves a careful balance of various strategies designed to transfer wealth efficiently and in accordance with the family's goals and values. Gifting, charitable contributions, and life insurance are key tools in this process, each offering unique benefits for wealth preservation and transfer. Regular review and adaptation of these strategies are crucial to ensure they remain aligned with changing family dynamics, financial goals, and tax laws.

Chapter 9: Advanced Portfolio Management Techniques

In the pursuit of optimal investment performance, advanced portfolio management techniques play a crucial role. This chapter delves into dynamic asset allocation, the use of stress testing and scenario analysis, and the importance of performance attribution and analysis. These techniques are vital for sophisticated investors seeking to enhance returns, manage risks, and understand the drivers of their portfolio's performance.

9.1 Dynamic Asset Allocation and Tactical Adjustments

- **Adapting to Market Changes:**
    - Dynamic asset allocation involves regularly adjusting the investment mix in response to short-term market fluctuations and changing economic conditions. This contrasts with a purely static, buy-and-hold strategy.
- **Tactical Portfolio Adjustments:**
    - Tactical adjustments are short-term changes made to capitalize on specific market opportunities or mitigate risks. These adjustments can include altering the asset class weightings, sector exposures, or geographic allocations in a portfolio.
- **Balancing Risk and Return:**
    - The goal of dynamic asset allocation and tactical

adjustments is to balance risk and return more effectively, taking into account the current market environment and economic forecasts.

9.2 Stress Testing and Scenario Analysis

- **Evaluating Potential Risks:**
    - Stress testing and scenario analysis involve simulating various market conditions and events to evaluate how they could impact a portfolio. This can help in understanding potential risks and the resilience of the portfolio under adverse conditions.
- **Scenario Planning:**
    - Different scenarios, such as market crashes, interest rate changes, or geopolitical events, are modeled to assess the potential impacts on portfolio performance. This helps in preparing contingency plans and strategies to mitigate these risks.

9.3 Performance Attribution and Analysis

- **Understanding Portfolio Drivers:**
    - Performance attribution is the process of analyzing the reasons behind a portfolio's performance. It helps in understanding which investments or decisions contributed positively or negatively to the overall results.
- **Analytical Insights:**
    - This analysis can provide insights into the effectiveness of investment strategies, asset allocation decisions, and individual security

selection. It is crucial for refining investment approaches and enhancing future portfolio performance.

- **Continuous Improvement:**
    - Regular performance analysis and attribution enable continuous improvement in investment strategy and decision-making processes. It also helps in aligning the portfolio more closely with the investor's objectives and risk tolerance.

In summary, Chapter 9 covers advanced portfolio management techniques essential for sophisticated investment management. Dynamic asset allocation, stress testing, and performance analysis are key tools for navigating complex markets, understanding portfolio performance, and making informed investment decisions. These techniques allow investors to adapt to changing market conditions, understand the risk profile of their portfolio, and systematically improve their investment approach for better outcomes.

9.1 Dynamic Asset Allocation and Tactical Adjustments

Dynamic asset allocation and tactical adjustments are crucial components of advanced portfolio management, enabling investors to navigate fluctuating markets and optimize their portfolios for changing economic conditions.

Adapting to Market Changes

- **Responsive Investment Strategy:**
  - Dynamic asset allocation is a proactive approach to portfolio management. It involves regularly reassessing and adjusting the composition of a portfolio in response to market movements and economic shifts, rather than adhering to a static asset mix.
- **Market Sensitivity:**
  - This strategy requires a keen understanding of market trends, economic indicators, and geopolitical events. It's about being agile and responsive, adapting the investment mix to current and anticipated market conditions.

Tactical Portfolio Adjustments

- **Short-Term Strategic Changes:**

    - Tactical adjustments are deliberate, short-term changes in the portfolio to seize specific market opportunities or to defend against potential risks.
- **Flexibility in Asset Allocation:**
    - These adjustments might involve shifting asset class weightings (e.g., from stocks to bonds), changing sector exposures (e.g., from technology to healthcare), or modifying geographic allocations (e.g., increasing investment in emerging markets).
- **Opportunistic and Protective Moves:**
    - Tactical moves can be opportunistic, aiming to exploit potential market gains, or protective, seeking to hedge against anticipated losses.

Balancing Risk and Return

- **Optimizing the Risk-Return Trade-Off:**
    - The overarching goal of dynamic asset allocation and tactical adjustments is to strike an optimal balance between risk and return. This balancing act is tailored to the investor's risk tolerance, investment time horizon, and financial goals.
- **Informed Decision Making:**
    - Effective implementation requires continuous monitoring of market conditions and the ability to make informed, data-driven decisions. It often involves a combination of quantitative analysis and qualitative judgment.
- **Aligning with Investment Objectives:**
    - Regular rebalancing ensures the portfolio remains aligned with the investor's objectives, taking into

account changing market dynamics and economic forecasts.

In conclusion, Chapter 9.1 emphasizes the importance of dynamic asset allocation and tactical adjustments in modern portfolio management. These strategies allow investors to adapt actively to market changes, capitalize on emerging opportunities, and manage risk in a systematic way. By continuously aligning the portfolio with the prevailing market conditions and individual investment objectives, dynamic asset allocation can enhance the potential for improved investment outcomes.

Adapting to Market Changes

Adapting to market changes through dynamic asset allocation is an essential strategy for advanced portfolio management. It involves a responsive and proactive approach, requiring an in-depth understanding of various market dynamics and the ability to adjust investment strategies accordingly.

Responsive Investment Strategy

- **Proactive Portfolio Management:**
    - Dynamic asset allocation contrasts sharply with a static, buy-and-hold strategy. It requires active engagement and continuous monitoring of the portfolio.
    - The approach involves regularly evaluating and adjusting the asset mix to align with current and projected market conditions, economic environments, and risk appetites.
- **Adaptability and Flexibility:**
    - This strategy demands adaptability. As markets evolve and economic scenarios change, the portfolio must be adjusted to either capitalize on emerging opportunities or mitigate potential risks.
    - The flexibility to shift the asset allocation enables investors to respond effectively to market corrections, rallies, or economic downturns.

Market Sensitivity

- **Understanding Market Dynamics:**
    - Successfully adapting to market changes necessitates a deep understanding of market trends, economic indicators, and geopolitical

developments.
    - This involves analyzing factors such as interest rate movements, inflation trends, political events, and global economic conditions, which can all have significant impacts on different asset classes.
- **Agility in Decision Making:**
    - The key to dynamic asset allocation is agility in decision-making. Investors must be able to interpret market signals and economic data quickly and accurately to make informed adjustments to their portfolios.
    - This requires staying abreast of market news, economic reports, and financial forecasts, as well as having the ability to discern short-term noise from genuine long-term trends.

In summary, adapting to market changes through dynamic asset allocation is a sophisticated approach that requires a blend of market knowledge, analytical skills, and agility in decision-making. This proactive strategy enables investors to optimize their portfolios in line with changing market conditions, enhancing the potential for better risk-adjusted returns. It underscores the importance of being flexible and responsive in the ever-changing landscape of the investment world.

Tactical Portfolio Adjustments

Tactical portfolio adjustments are a key element of dynamic asset allocation, allowing investors to make short-term strategic changes in response to evolving market conditions. These adjustments are designed to either capitalize on immediate market opportunities or to protect the portfolio from potential risks.

Short-Term Strategic Changes

- **Targeted Adjustments for Market Conditions:**
  - Tactical adjustments are precise and targeted changes made to the portfolio to adapt to short-term market scenarios. These changes are usually based on current market analysis and short-term forecasts.
- **Responsiveness to Market Signals:**
  - The effectiveness of tactical adjustments depends on the ability to quickly and accurately respond to market signals. This includes interpreting economic data, market trends, and geopolitical events that could influence investment returns.

Flexibility in Asset Allocation

- **Adapting Asset Mix:**
  - Tactical adjustments offer the flexibility to shift the asset mix of the portfolio. This could involve reallocating investments from one asset class to another, like moving from stocks to bonds in a volatile or declining stock market.
- **Sector and Geographic Rebalancing:**
  - These adjustments can also include changing exposures to different sectors or geographies based on market outlook. For instance, reducing

exposure to a particular industry that might be facing regulatory challenges or increasing investment in emerging markets due to growth potential.

Opportunistic and Protective Moves

- **Capitalizing on Opportunities:**
    - Tactical moves can be opportunistic, aiming to take advantage of potential short-term market gains. This could include investing in undervalued sectors or assets poised for a rebound.
- **Risk Mitigation:**
    - Conversely, they can be protective, designed to shield the portfolio from anticipated market downturns or risks. This could involve strategies like hedging or increasing the allocation to defensive assets.

In conclusion, tactical portfolio adjustments are an essential component of a comprehensive investment strategy, providing the agility to respond to short-term market fluctuations. These adjustments allow investors to both seize timely opportunities and mitigate potential risks, contributing to the overall resilience and performance of the portfolio. The success of tactical adjustments hinges on a thorough understanding of market dynamics and the agility to make informed decisions.

Balancing Risk and Return

In advanced portfolio management, balancing risk and return is crucial for achieving long-term investment success. Dynamic asset allocation and tactical adjustments are key strategies used to optimize this balance, ensuring that the portfolio aligns with the investor's objectives and market realities.

Optimizing the Risk-Return Trade-Off

- **Tailoring to Investor Profiles:**
    - The process of balancing risk and return is highly individualized, depending on each investor's risk tolerance, investment horizon, and specific financial goals.
    - An investor with a higher risk tolerance might lean towards a portfolio with a greater allocation to equities or other high-risk assets, while a more risk-averse investor might prefer a higher allocation to bonds or other fixed-income securities.
- **Risk-Return Considerations:**
    - The goal is to achieve the highest possible return for a given level of risk. This involves not only selecting the right mix of assets but also understanding how different investments interact within the portfolio to affect overall risk and return.

Informed Decision Making

- **Continuous Market Monitoring:**
    - Effectively balancing risk and return requires ongoing monitoring of market conditions. This includes keeping abreast of economic trends,

market developments, and geopolitical events that could influence investment performance.

- **Data-Driven Strategies:**
    - Decisions should be based on a combination of quantitative analysis (such as statistical models and financial metrics) and qualitative judgment (like market sentiment and economic forecasts).
- **Adaptive Strategies:**
    - The ability to adapt the investment strategy in response to market changes is key. This may involve increasing or decreasing risk exposure based on market cycles or economic indicators.

Aligning with Investment Objectives

- **Regular Portfolio Rebalancing:**
    - Regular rebalancing is essential to maintain the desired asset allocation over time. This process adjusts the portfolio to remain in line with the investor's risk tolerance and investment goals.
- **Responsive to Changes:**
    - Rebalancing also involves responding to significant changes in the market or in the investor's life, such as a change in income, risk tolerance, or investment time horizon.

In summary, Chapter 9.1 underlines the importance of balancing risk and return through dynamic asset allocation and tactical adjustments. This strategy involves tailoring the investment approach to individual risk profiles, continuously monitoring market conditions, and making informed decisions based on both data and market insights. Regular rebalancing ensures that the portfolio remains in alignment with the investor's objectives, even as market dynamics and personal circumstances evolve. This balanced approach is crucial for navigating the complexities of the investment landscape and achieving long-term financial objectives.

9.2 Stress Testing and Scenario Analysis

Stress testing and scenario analysis are vital tools in advanced portfolio management, allowing investors to evaluate the resilience of their portfolios under various hypothetical conditions. These techniques are essential for understanding and mitigating potential risks.

Evaluating Potential Risks

- **Simulating Adverse Market Conditions:**
    - Stress testing involves creating hypothetical adverse market scenarios to evaluate how a portfolio might perform under such conditions. This could include extreme market volatility, economic recessions, or other financial crises.
- **Assessing Portfolio Resilience:**
    - The aim is to assess the robustness of the portfolio against these stress scenarios. It helps in identifying potential vulnerabilities in the investment strategy and testing the portfolio's capacity to withstand market shocks.
- **Risk Management Tool:**
    - Stress testing is a proactive risk management tool. By anticipating how different types of risks could impact the portfolio, investors can make informed decisions to strengthen their investment

approach.

Scenario Planning

- **Modeling Various Market Events:**
    - Scenario analysis extends beyond stress testing by considering a broader range of potential events, including both negative and positive developments. This could involve modeling the effects of various scenarios like significant interest rate changes, geopolitical upheavals, or technological breakthroughs.
- **Understanding Impact on Portfolio Performance:**
    - Different scenarios are used to evaluate how each might affect the performance of the portfolio. This analysis provides insights into which assets or strategies are more sensitive to certain types of risks.
- **Developing Contingency Plans:**
    - The insights gained from scenario analysis are used to develop contingency plans. These plans outline strategies to mitigate potential risks or capitalize on possible opportunities presented by different market events.
- **Strategic Adjustments:**
    - Based on scenario analysis, strategic adjustments can be made to the portfolio. This might involve diversifying investments, adjusting asset allocations, or implementing hedging strategies to protect against adverse outcomes.

In conclusion, Chapter 9.2 highlights the importance of stress testing and scenario analysis in modern portfolio management. These techniques allow investors to proactively evaluate and manage risks by understanding how different market conditions and events could impact their portfolios. By preparing for a range of potential scenarios, investors can enhance the resilience of their portfolios, better positioning them to withstand market uncertainties and capitalize on emerging opportunities.

Evaluating Potential Risks

Evaluating potential risks through stress testing is an essential practice in advanced portfolio management. It involves simulating adverse market conditions to gauge how a portfolio might perform, thereby enabling investors to understand and prepare for potential risks.

Simulating Adverse Market Conditions

- **Creating Hypothetical Scenarios:**
    - Stress testing involves constructing various hypothetical scenarios that represent adverse market conditions. These scenarios could encompass a wide range of events, from extreme market volatility and steep declines in asset prices to economic recessions or financial crises.
- **Testing Portfolio Performance:**
    - The purpose of these simulations is to evaluate how the portfolio might perform under such challenging conditions. This includes examining the impact on asset values, liquidity, and overall portfolio stability.

Assessing Portfolio Resilience

- **Identifying Vulnerabilities:**
    - Stress testing helps in identifying potential vulnerabilities within the portfolio. This could reveal concentrations in certain assets or sectors that may be particularly susceptible to market downturns or specific economic events.
- **Testing Capacity to Withstand Shocks:**
    - The process evaluates the portfolio's capacity to withstand market shocks. This assessment is

crucial in understanding whether the current investment strategy is aligned with the investor's risk tolerance and investment objectives.

Risk Management Tool

- **Proactive Approach to Risk Management:**
    - Stress testing serves as a proactive risk management tool. By simulating adverse conditions, it allows investors to anticipate and prepare for how different types of risks could materially impact their investments.
- **Informed Decision Making:**
    - Armed with the insights from stress testing, investors can make informed decisions to modify or strengthen their investment strategies. This might involve diversifying the portfolio, adjusting asset allocations, or implementing strategies to hedge against specific risks.

In summary, Chapter 9.2 emphasizes the importance of stress testing as a critical component of risk management in portfolio management. By simulating adverse market conditions and evaluating the resilience of the portfolio, investors can identify potential risks and vulnerabilities, and take proactive steps to mitigate these risks. This approach enables investors to build more robust and resilient investment strategies, better equipped to handle the complexities and uncertainties of the financial markets.

Scenario Planning

Scenario planning is a comprehensive approach in portfolio management, encompassing a wide range of potential market events. It goes beyond stress testing by considering both positive and negative developments and their potential impacts on a portfolio.

Modeling Various Market Events

- **Broad Range of Scenarios:**
    - Scenario analysis involves modeling the effects of various potential market events, which can range from economic changes like interest rate fluctuations to geopolitical upheavals and technological innovations.
- **Diverse Impact Analysis:**
    - The scenarios modeled are diverse, encompassing both risks and opportunities. This approach helps in preparing for a wide array of possibilities, rather than focusing solely on adverse conditions.

Understanding Impact on Portfolio Performance

- **Performance Under Different Conditions:**
    - Each scenario is used to evaluate how it might affect the portfolio's performance. This analysis is crucial in understanding the sensitivity of different assets or strategies to various types of risks or opportunities.
- **Identifying Sensitive Areas:**
    - Scenario planning can reveal which portions of the portfolio are more vulnerable or responsive to certain market conditions, enabling more informed investment decisions.

Developing Contingency Plans

- **Preparing for Various Outcomes:**
    - Insights from scenario analysis are instrumental in developing contingency plans. These plans are designed to address potential risks or to take advantage of opportunities that may arise from specific market events.
- **Flexibility and Preparedness:**
    - Having contingency plans in place ensures that the investor is prepared to act swiftly and effectively, regardless of market conditions.

Strategic Adjustments

- **Proactive Portfolio Management:**
    - Based on the insights gained from scenario analysis, investors can make strategic adjustments to their portfolios. These adjustments might include diversifying investments to reduce risk exposure or reallocating assets to capitalize on potential market opportunities.
- **Implementing Risk Mitigation Strategies:**
    - In some cases, implementing hedging strategies or other risk mitigation techniques might be necessary to protect the portfolio from possible adverse scenarios.

In summary, Chapter 9.2 highlights the importance of scenario planning as a critical element of advanced portfolio management. By considering a broad range of potential market events and their impacts on portfolio performance, scenario planning enables investors to prepare comprehensive contingency plans and make strategic adjustments. This proactive approach to portfolio management enhances the investor's ability to navigate complex market environments, mitigate risks, and seize potential opportunities.

9.3 Performance Attribution and Analysis

Performance attribution and analysis are integral components of advanced portfolio management. They involve dissecting the portfolio's performance to understand the factors contributing to its success or underperformance. This process is vital for refining investment strategies and aligning the portfolio with the investor's goals.

Understanding Portfolio Drivers

- **Analyzing Performance Contributors:**
  - Performance attribution is a detailed analysis aimed at pinpointing the specific investments or decisions that have contributed to the portfolio's overall performance. This includes assessing the impact of asset allocation, security selection, and market timing.
- **Identifying Success and Failure Factors:**
  - By understanding what worked and what didn't, investors gain valuable insights into the effectiveness of their investment strategies. This might reveal, for instance, whether outperformance was due to a particular sector's strong performance or effective stock picks within that sector.

Analytical Insights

- **Evaluating Investment Strategies:**
    - Performance analysis provides insights into how different aspects of the investment strategy have played out. It evaluates how asset allocation decisions and individual security selections have contributed to the portfolio's risk and return profile.
- **Informing Future Decisions:**
    - The insights gained are crucial for refining future investment approaches. They help in determining whether to maintain certain strategies, adjust asset allocations, or change investment focus.

Continuous Improvement

- **Enhancing Investment Strategy:**
    - Regular performance analysis and attribution are essential for continuous improvement. They allow investors to adapt their strategies based on what has been effective and to address any shortcomings identified.
- **Alignment with Objectives and Risk Tolerance:**
    - Ongoing analysis ensures that the investment strategy remains aligned with the investor's objectives and risk tolerance. As these factors can change over time, consistent review and adjustment of the portfolio are necessary.
- **Benchmarking Performance:**
    - Comparing the portfolio's performance against relevant benchmarks is also a part of this process.

This comparison helps in assessing how well the portfolio is doing in the context of broader market trends.

In summary, Chapter 9.3 underscores the importance of performance attribution and analysis in portfolio management. This process is key to understanding the drivers of portfolio performance and provides the basis for making informed decisions to enhance future results. Regular and thorough analysis of performance helps in continuously refining investment strategies, ensuring they remain effective and aligned with the investor's evolving goals and risk profile.

Understanding Portfolio Drivers

Gaining a deep understanding of the factors driving a portfolio's performance is crucial for effective investment management. Performance attribution analysis serves this purpose by dissecting the portfolio's returns and identifying the key contributors to its success or underperformance.

Analyzing Performance Contributors

- **Dissecting Portfolio Performance:**
    - Performance attribution involves a detailed examination of how various elements of the investment strategy have influenced the overall results. It's about breaking down the portfolio's performance into its constituent parts for a clearer understanding.
- **Impact of Asset Allocation and Security Selection:**
    - The analysis looks at how decisions regarding asset allocation and individual security selection have affected performance. It also considers the role of market timing - the impact of decisions about when to buy or sell assets.
- **Quantitative and Qualitative Aspects:**
    - The attribution process includes both quantitative analysis (like statistical performance measures) and qualitative assessments (such as the rationale behind investment choices).

Identifying Success and Failure Factors

- **Learning from Outcomes:**
    - Understanding what elements of the portfolio worked well and which did not is key to refining future investment strategies. This analysis can

provide valuable lessons for both successful and unsuccessful investment decisions.

- **Sector and Security Performance:**
    - For instance, if the portfolio outperformed, was it because a particular sector did exceptionally well, or was it due to selecting the right stocks within a moderately performing sector? Conversely, underperformance might be attributed to poor sector selection or unsuccessful stock picks.
- **Insights into Strategy Effectiveness:**
    - Analyzing the reasons behind the performance helps investors gauge the effectiveness of their strategies. It's crucial for understanding whether the investment approach aligns with the portfolio's objectives and risk tolerance.

In conclusion, understanding the drivers of portfolio performance through detailed attribution analysis is essential for informed investment management. It allows investors to identify the strengths and weaknesses of their strategies, providing a basis for continuous improvement. This analysis helps in aligning future investment decisions with the overarching investment goals and risk parameters, ultimately leading to more sophisticated and successful portfolio management.

Analytical Insights

Gaining analytical insights from performance analysis is a pivotal aspect of advanced portfolio management. It involves a thorough evaluation of various investment strategies and their outcomes, providing a foundation for making informed future investment decisions.

Evaluating Investment Strategies

- **Assessment of Strategy Execution:**
    - Performance analysis looks at how the executed investment strategies have fared over time. It assesses the effectiveness of asset allocation decisions and the impact of specific security selections on the portfolio's overall risk and return.
- **Risk-Return Contribution:**
    - This analysis helps in understanding how different investments within the portfolio have contributed to or detracted from its risk and return. It can highlight which assets or strategies were key drivers of performance and which were less effective or even detrimental.
- **Comprehensive Strategy Review:**
    - The process involves reviewing both successful and underperforming strategies. This comprehensive approach ensures a balanced view of the portfolio's performance, considering various market conditions and investment periods.

Informing Future Decisions

- **Refining Investment Approaches:**
    - The insights derived from performance analysis are instrumental in refining future investment strategies. They provide a clear understanding of what strategies worked, which can be replicated or enhanced, and what strategies failed, which might need reconsideration or elimination.
- **Decision-Making for Asset Allocation:**
    - Based on the analysis, decisions can be made

about whether to maintain the current asset allocation, adjust the proportions of different asset classes, or shift the focus to new areas. For instance, if certain asset classes or sectors consistently underperform or contribute excessively to portfolio volatility, they might be reduced or replaced.

- **Adapting to Changing Market Conditions:**
  - The insights also help in adapting investment strategies to changing market conditions. Understanding past performance in various market environments can guide how to position the portfolio for future conditions.

In summary, the analytical insights gained from performance attribution and analysis are invaluable for effective portfolio management. They enable investors to evaluate the impact of their investment strategies and make informed decisions for future asset allocation and security selection. This ongoing process of analysis and refinement is crucial for aligning the portfolio with the investor's objectives and adapting to the dynamic nature of the financial markets.

Continuous Improvement

Continuous improvement in portfolio management is a dynamic process, requiring regular performance analysis and adjustments. It's about refining the investment strategy over time, ensuring alignment with changing objectives, and benchmarking performance to understand its context within broader market trends.

Enhancing Investment Strategy

- **Adaptive Investment Approaches:**
    - Regular performance reviews allow investors to adapt their strategies based on past effectiveness. This involves identifying successful elements of the strategy and replicating or expanding them, while also addressing and rectifying any shortcomings.
- **Learning and Evolving:**
    - Continuous improvement is based on learning from both successes and failures. It's about evolving the investment approach to incorporate new insights, market conditions, and investment techniques.

Alignment with Objectives and Risk Tolerance

- **Staying in Sync with Goals:**
    - As an investor's financial goals, life circumstances, and risk tolerance can change over time, it's crucial that the investment strategy adapts accordingly. Regular analysis ensures the strategy remains relevant and aligned with the current objectives.
- **Dynamic Risk Management:**

- Risk tolerance is not static; it evolves with market conditions, economic cycles, and personal life stages. Continuous analysis allows for adjustments in the portfolio to align with the current risk profile of the investor.

Benchmarking Performance

- **Measuring Against Benchmarks:**
    - Comparing the portfolio's performance against relevant benchmarks is an important part of continuous improvement. This comparison provides context, showing how the portfolio is performing relative to broader market indices or sector-specific benchmarks.
- **Contextualizing Performance:**
    - Benchmarking helps in understanding whether the portfolio's performance is due to market-wide trends or specific investment decisions. It provides a framework to evaluate the effectiveness of the investment strategy against a relevant standard.

In conclusion, Chapter 9.3 emphasizes the importance of continuous improvement in portfolio management. Regular performance analysis, alignment with changing objectives and risk tolerance, and benchmarking against relevant standards are key to refining and enhancing the investment strategy. This ongoing process ensures that the portfolio remains effective, responsive to market changes, and aligned

Chapter 10: The Future of Investing

In the ever-evolving landscape of investing, staying abreast of future trends, technological advancements, and global economic shifts is crucial for advanced investors. Chapter 10 delves into the future of investing, highlighting emerging technologies, global economic trends, and the importance of continuous learning and adaptation.

10.1 Emerging Technologies and Investment Opportunities

- **Technology-Driven Investment Landscape:**
    - This section explores how emerging technologies are reshaping investment opportunities. It covers advancements like blockchain, artificial intelligence (AI), machine learning, and big data analytics, and their implications for investors.
- **Innovative Financial Instruments:**
    - Discussion includes new financial products and services spawned by technological innovation, such as digital currencies, robo-advisors, and automated trading systems.
- **Sectoral Impacts and Opportunities:**
    - The impact of technological advancements on different sectors and how these create new investment opportunities or risks is also examined.

10.2 Global Economic Trends and Market Predictions

- **Navigating Global Economic Changes:**
    - This part discusses the importance of understanding and responding to global economic trends, such as shifts in trade policies, international relations, and demographic changes.
- **Predictive Analysis for Market Trends:**
    - Utilizing various tools and models for predictive analysis to anticipate market movements and economic shifts. This includes examining emerging markets, changing consumer behaviors, and environmental, social, and governance (ESG) trends.

10.3 Continuous Learning and Adaptation for the Advanced Investor

- **Commitment to Lifelong Learning:**
    - Emphasizing the need for continuous learning to keep pace with the rapidly changing investment landscape. This includes staying updated with the latest research, market developments, and investment theories.
- **Adapting Investment Strategies:**
    - The importance of being flexible and willing to adapt investment strategies in response to new information, market changes, and emerging trends.
- **Utilizing Resources and Networks:**
    - Encouraging the use of a wide range of resources, including educational platforms, professional

networks, and financial advisors, to gain diverse perspectives and insights.

Chapter 10 presents a forward-looking view on the landscape of investing, focusing on the impact of emerging technologies, global economic trends, and the necessity for continuous learning and adaptation. Understanding these elements is crucial for advanced investors seeking to navigate the complexities of the future investment environment successfully.

10.1 Emerging Technologies and Investment Opportunities

In the rapidly evolving world of finance, emerging technologies are playing a pivotal role in shaping new investment opportunities. This section delves into how these technological advancements are transforming the investment landscape, offering innovative financial instruments, and impacting various sectors.

Technology-Driven Investment Landscape

- **Impact of Blockchain and AI:**
    - Blockchain technology is revolutionizing areas such as transaction processing and asset tracking, offering enhanced security and transparency.
    - Artificial Intelligence (AI) and Machine Learning are transforming investment analysis and decision-making processes, enabling more sophisticated predictive models and personalized investment solutions.
- **Big Data in Investment:**
    - The proliferation of Big Data analytics has opened new avenues for analyzing market trends and consumer behaviors, offering deeper insights and aiding in more informed investment decisions.

Innovative Financial Instruments

- **Digital Currencies and Assets:**
    - The rise of digital currencies, including cryptocurrencies, is creating a new asset class. These digital assets present both unique opportunities and risks, necessitating a deep understanding of their market dynamics.
- **Robo-Advisors and Automation:**
    - Technological innovation has led to the development of robo-advisors, which use algorithms to offer investment advice and portfolio management with minimal human intervention.
    - Automated trading systems are becoming increasingly sophisticated, enabling high-speed and high-efficiency trading strategies.

Sectoral Impacts and Opportunities

- **Sector-Specific Changes:**
    - Technologies like AI, blockchain, and IoT (Internet of Things) are having profound impacts across various sectors, from finance and healthcare to manufacturing and retail.
- **Emergence of New Investment Opportunities:**
    - These technological shifts are creating new investment opportunities in emerging sectors and companies at the forefront of innovation.
- **Risk Consideration:**
    - With these opportunities also come risks, particularly related to the adoption rate of new technologies, regulatory changes, and market acceptance. Investors need to carefully assess these

risks when exploring investments in technology-driven sectors.

Chapter 10.1 highlights how emerging technologies are not only creating new investment opportunities but also changing the traditional dynamics of various sectors. For the advanced investor, staying informed about these technological advancements and understanding their implications is crucial for identifying new growth areas and managing associated risks. The intersection of technology and finance is continuously evolving, offering both exciting opportunities and new challenges in the investment world.

Technology-Driven Investment Landscape

The investment landscape is rapidly evolving with the advent of groundbreaking technologies like blockchain, artificial intelligence (AI), and big data analytics. These technologies are not just transforming existing processes but also paving the way for entirely new strategies and tools in investment management.

Impact of Blockchain and AI

- **Blockchain Technology:**
    - Blockchain is altering the financial industry landscape, particularly in areas like transaction processing, asset tracking, and securities settlement. Its decentralized nature offers enhanced security and transparency, reducing the risk of fraud and errors.
    - The technology is also fostering innovations in areas such as smart contracts and tokenization of assets, which could revolutionize traditional investment vehicles.
- **Artificial Intelligence and Machine Learning:**
    - AI and machine learning are redefining investment analysis and decision-making. By processing vast amounts of data at incredible speeds, these technologies enable the development of more sophisticated predictive models.
    - They facilitate personalized investment solutions and automated decision-making processes, allowing for more dynamic and responsive portfolio management.

Big Data in Investment

- **Harnessing Data for Insights:**
  - The proliferation of big data analytics has dramatically enhanced the capability to analyze complex market trends and consumer behaviors. This abundance of data, when harnessed effectively, can provide deeper insights into market dynamics.
- **Informed Decision-Making:**
  - Big data enables investors to make more informed decisions by providing a more nuanced understanding of the market. It can identify hidden patterns, correlations, and trends that traditional analysis methods might miss.
- **Risk Management:**
  - Big data also plays a crucial role in risk management. By analyzing market and economic data, investors can better understand potential risks and devise strategies to mitigate them.

In conclusion, Chapter 10.1 underscores the profound impact of emerging technologies on the investment landscape. Blockchain, AI, and big data analytics are not only enhancing existing investment processes but also creating new opportunities and challenges. For investors, staying abreast of these technological advancements and understanding their applications in finance is critical for navigating the future of investing. These technologies offer the potential for more secure, efficient, and tailored investment solutions, but they also require a new level of technological understanding and adaptability.

Innovative Financial Instruments

The integration of technology into finance has led to the emergence of innovative financial instruments, reshaping the way investors interact with the market. Digital currencies and automated investment platforms are at the forefront of this transformation.

Digital Currencies and Assets

- **Emergence of a New Asset Class:**
  - Digital currencies, including cryptocurrencies like Bitcoin and Ethereum, have emerged as a new asset class. They represent a significant shift from traditional financial systems, offering decentralization, digital ledger technology, and often, limited regulatory oversight.
- **Unique Opportunities and Challenges:**
  - Investing in digital currencies presents unique opportunities due to their high growth potential and increasing acceptance. However, they also pose significant risks, including high volatility, regulatory uncertainty, and security concerns.
- **Understanding Market Dynamics:**
  - To effectively invest in digital currencies, a deep understanding of their market dynamics, underlying technology, and regulatory landscape is crucial. Investors need to stay informed about technological advancements and regulatory developments in this area.

Robo-Advisors and Automation

- **Rise of Algorithmic Advice:**
  - Robo-advisors are automated platforms that provide investment advice and portfolio

management services using algorithms. They have democratized access to investment advice, making it more accessible and affordable.

- **Efficiency and Customization:**
    - These platforms typically offer efficient and customized portfolio management based on the individual investor's goals, risk tolerance, and time horizon. They use algorithms to optimize asset allocation and rebalance portfolios as needed.
- **Sophistication in Automated Trading:**
    - Automated trading systems have become more advanced, capable of executing high-speed and complex trading strategies. They use algorithms to analyze market data, execute trades at optimal times, and exploit market inefficiencies.
- **Impact on Market Dynamics:**
    - The increasing use of automated trading systems and algorithm-based decision-making is influencing market dynamics. It's essential for investors to understand the impact of these technologies on market volatility and pricing.

In conclusion, Chapter 10.1 highlights the significant impact of technological advancements on financial instruments. The rise of digital currencies and automated investment platforms, such as robo-advisors and sophisticated trading systems, represent a paradigm shift in the investment world. While they offer new opportunities for growth and efficiency, they also require investors to have a comprehensive understanding of their mechanisms, risks, and implications in the broader financial landscape. Adapting to these innovations is crucial for investors looking to stay competitive and successful in the rapidly evolving world of finance.

Sectoral Impacts and Opportunities

The advent of emerging technologies such as AI, blockchain, and the Internet of Things (IoT) is bringing about transformative changes across various sectors. This evolution is creating new investment opportunities, but it also introduces specific risks that need careful consideration.

Sector-Specific Changes

- **Widespread Technological Impact:**
  - AI is revolutionizing sectors like finance, where it's used for predictive analytics, and healthcare, for diagnostic and treatment advancements. In manufacturing, AI and IoT are integral to the development of smart factories and automation.
- **Blockchain Beyond Finance:**
  - While blockchain is predominantly associated with finance, its impact extends to sectors like supply chain management, where it offers enhanced transparency and traceability, and even to digital identity verification systems.
- **IoT Integration:**
  - The IoT is transforming retail and consumer goods industries by enhancing customer engagement and optimizing supply chain operations. It's also playing a crucial role in smart city developments and energy management.

Emergence of New Investment Opportunities

- **Investing in Innovation:**
  - These technological advancements are opening doors to investment opportunities in emerging sectors and innovative companies. For instance,

investments in fintech, healthtech, or green technology can offer exposure to cutting-edge developments.

- **Venture Capital and Startups:**
    - The surge in startups focused on leveraging these technologies presents potential investment opportunities, particularly through venture capital.

Risk Consideration

- **Assessing Adoption and Implementation Risks:**
    - When investing in sectors driven by new technologies, it's crucial to consider the adoption rate and the practicality of implementation. Some technologies may face hurdles in widespread adoption due to cost, complexity, or consumer resistance.
- **Regulatory Landscape:**
    - The regulatory environment for new technologies can be uncertain and rapidly evolving. Changes in regulations or compliance requirements can significantly impact the viability and profitability of investments in these sectors.
- **Market Acceptance:**
    - Understanding market acceptance and consumer behavior is key. Technologies that fail to gain market traction can pose risks to investors.

In conclusion, Chapter 10.1 emphasizes the importance of understanding the sectoral impacts and opportunities presented by emerging technologies. While these advancements offer exciting new avenues for investment, they also come with unique challenges and risks. Investors need to stay informed about technological trends, assess the potential for market adoption, and consider the regulatory environment when exploring these opportunities. Being cognizant of these factors is crucial for making informed investment decisions in technology-driven sectors.

10.2 Global Economic Trends and Market Predictions

In an increasingly interconnected world, understanding and navigating global economic trends is crucial for advanced investors. This section delves into how shifts in trade policies, international relations, demographic changes, and other global factors influence market dynamics and investment strategies.

Navigating Global Economic Changes

- **Impact of Trade and International Relations:**
    - Trade policies and international relations can have significant impacts on global markets. Changes in tariffs, trade agreements, or geopolitical tensions can affect industries, currencies, and entire economies.
- **Demographic Shifts:**
    - Global demographic changes, such as aging populations in some countries and youthful demographics in others, can influence market trends. These shifts impact labor markets, consumer spending patterns, and healthcare needs, among other sectors.
- **Cultural and Social Changes:**
    - Cultural and social dynamics, including changing consumer preferences and behaviors, also play a

crucial role in shaping market trends. These factors can drive growth in certain industries while leading to declines in others.

Predictive Analysis for Market Trends

- **Leveraging Predictive Tools:**
    - Predictive analysis involves using various tools and models to forecast market movements and economic trends. This includes statistical models, AI algorithms, and market sentiment analysis.
- **Focus on Emerging Markets:**
    - Keeping an eye on emerging markets is key, as these regions often present high-growth opportunities. Understanding the economic, political, and cultural contexts of these markets is essential for accurate predictions and effective investment strategies.
- **ESG Considerations:**
    - Environmental, Social, and Governance (ESG) trends are increasingly important in predicting market trends. Investors are focusing more on sustainability and social impact, which can drive investment decisions and corporate behaviors.
- **Adapting to Economic Cycles:**
    - Understanding economic cycles and their implications on different asset classes helps in making more informed investment decisions. This includes recognizing signs of economic recovery, stagnation, or recession.

In conclusion, Chapter 10.2 highlights the importance of understanding and responding to global economic trends for effective investment management. Keeping abreast of international developments, demographic shifts, and ESG trends is crucial for anticipating market movements and making informed investment decisions. Utilizing predictive analysis tools and models enhances the ability to navigate these complex and ever-changing global economic landscapes.

Navigating Global Economic Changes

Understanding and navigating global economic changes are critical for investors looking to make informed decisions in an interconnected world economy. This section explores how trade policies, international relations, demographic shifts, and cultural changes can significantly impact global markets and investment strategies.

Impact of Trade and International Relations

- **Trade Policy Influence:**
    - Changes in trade policies, such as the imposition or removal of tariffs, can dramatically affect industries by altering their cost structures and market access. These changes can influence the competitiveness of companies and sectors on a global scale.
- **International Relations and Geopolitics:**
    - Geopolitical tensions and international relations play a significant role in financial markets. Conflicts or collaborations between countries can lead to fluctuations in commodity prices, currency values, and investment flows into and out of regions or countries.
- **Economic Alliances and Agreements:**
    - New trade agreements or changes in existing ones can open up or restrict opportunities for businesses and investors. These agreements can redefine supply chains and market accessibility.

Demographic Shifts

- **Aging Populations:**
    - In countries with aging populations, there's likely

to be increased demand in sectors like healthcare, pharmaceuticals, and retirement services. This demographic trend can also have implications for labor markets and economic growth rates.

- **Youthful Demographics:**
    - Conversely, countries with younger populations might experience different economic dynamics, such as higher potential for workforce growth and evolving consumer markets, which can drive demand in sectors like technology, education, and entertainment.

Cultural and Social Changes

- **Consumer Preferences and Behaviors:**
    - Cultural and social changes, including shifts in consumer preferences and behaviors, can significantly impact market trends. This includes trends like increased focus on sustainability, wellness, and digital consumption.
- **Industry Growth or Decline:**
    - These cultural shifts can lead to growth in certain industries (like renewable energy or digital services) and decline in others (such as traditional retail or fossil fuels).
- **Adapting to Consumer Trends:**
    - Investors need to be attuned to these cultural and social dynamics to identify emerging opportunities and potential risks in different sectors.

In conclusion, navigating global economic changes requires investors to have a comprehensive understanding of various factors that shape market dynamics. Trade policies, international relations, demographic trends, and cultural shifts all play crucial roles in influencing global markets. By staying informed and adaptive to these changes, investors can better position their portfolios to capitalize on emerging opportunities and mitigate potential risks in a rapidly evolving global economy.

Predictive Analysis for Market Trends

Predictive analysis for market trends is an essential aspect of modern investment strategy. It involves utilizing various analytical tools and models to anticipate future market movements and economic trends. This approach enables investors to make more informed and strategic investment decisions.

Leveraging Predictive Tools

- **Advanced Analytical Models:**
    - Utilizing statistical models, AI algorithms, and market sentiment analysis tools are key components of predictive analysis. These tools process vast amounts of data to identify patterns, trends, and potential market movements.
- **AI and Machine Learning:**
    - AI and machine learning algorithms are particularly effective in parsing complex market data and extracting actionable insights. They can adjust to new information and refine their predictions over time.

Focus on Emerging Markets

- **Identifying Opportunities in Growth Regions:**
    - Emerging markets often present unique high-growth opportunities. Paying attention to these markets is crucial for investors looking to diversify and capitalize on rapid economic development.
- **Contextual Understanding:**
    - Accurate predictions in emerging markets require a deep understanding of local economic, political, and cultural contexts. This knowledge helps in assessing the viability and potential of investment

opportunities in these regions.

ESG Considerations

- **Importance of Sustainability:**
    - Environmental, Social, and Governance (ESG) considerations are increasingly becoming a focus in investment decision-making. They play a significant role in predicting long-term market trends and company performance.
- **Impact on Corporate Performance:**
    - Companies with strong ESG practices are often seen as better positioned for long-term success. This makes ESG analysis an important tool for predicting future market leaders and industry trends.

Adapting to Economic Cycles

- **Understanding Market Phases:**
    - Recognizing and understanding different phases of economic cycles is crucial for predictive analysis. Each phase – recovery, growth, stagnation, or recession – has distinct characteristics and implications for various asset classes.
- **Cyclical Investment Strategies:**
    - By understanding these cycles, investors can adapt their strategies to maximize returns in different economic conditions. For example, certain sectors may perform better during economic recoveries, while others may be more resilient during downturns.

In conclusion, Chapter 10.2 emphasizes the significance of predictive analysis in understanding market trends and making informed investment decisions. Leveraging advanced tools, focusing on emerging markets, incorporating ESG considerations, and adapting to economic cycles are key to navigating the complex landscape of global investing. This approach enables investors to anticipate market changes and align their strategies accordingly, positioning them for potential growth and success in a dynamic economic environment.

10.3 Continuous Learning and Adaptation for the Advanced Investor

In the dynamic world of investing, continuous learning and adaptation are key for advanced investors to remain effective and competitive. Chapter 10.3 underscores the importance of lifelong learning, flexibility in investment strategies, and the utilization of various resources to stay informed and responsive to market changes.

Commitment to Lifelong Learning

- **Keeping Pace with Market Evolution:**
    - The investment landscape is continually evolving, driven by technological advancements, economic shifts, and changing regulatory environments. Staying abreast of these changes requires a commitment to ongoing education and research.
- **Engaging with Latest Research and Developments:**
    - This involves regularly engaging with the latest market research, economic analyses, and evolving investment theories. Keeping up-to-date with financial news, academic studies, and industry reports is crucial for informed decision-making.
- **Educational Platforms and Continuous Training:**
    - Utilizing various educational platforms, attending seminars, webinars, and industry conferences are effective ways to stay informed and enhance one's

knowledge base.

Adapting Investment Strategies

- **Flexibility and Responsiveness:**
    - The ability to adapt investment strategies in response to new information and changing market conditions is critical. This flexibility allows investors to capitalize on emerging opportunities and mitigate potential risks.
- **Revising Strategies Based on Market Dynamics:**
    - Regularly reviewing and revising investment strategies ensures they remain aligned with current market dynamics and personal investment goals.

Utilizing Resources and Networks

- **Leveraging Diverse Perspectives:**
    - Accessing a wide range of resources, including educational platforms, investment tools, and professional networks, provides a broader perspective on market trends and investment strategies.
- **Professional Networks and Financial Advisors:**
    - Building a strong professional network and consulting with financial advisors can offer valuable insights and alternative viewpoints. These relationships can be instrumental in identifying new opportunities and avoiding common pitfalls.
- **Community Engagement and Forums:**
    - Participating in investment forums and community discussions can also be beneficial.

These platforms provide a space for sharing ideas, strategies, and experiences with other investors.

In summary, Chapter 10.3 emphasizes the necessity for advanced investors to engage in continuous learning and adapt their strategies to the ever-changing investment landscape. Staying informed, being flexible, and leveraging diverse resources and networks are fundamental to maintaining a competitive edge in the complex world of investing. This approach not only enhances investment acumen but also contributes to better decision-making and improved investment outcomes.

Commitment to Lifelong Learning

In the dynamic realm of investing, a commitment to lifelong learning is essential for staying relevant and making informed decisions. This section highlights the importance of keeping pace with the ever-evolving market landscape, engaging with the latest research and developments, and continuously enhancing one's knowledge through various educational resources.

Keeping Pace with Market Evolution

- **Adapting to Changes:**
    - The investment landscape is in a state of constant flux, influenced by rapid technological advancements, economic shifts, and evolving regulatory frameworks. Adapting to these changes is crucial for maintaining a competitive edge.
- **Understanding New Developments:**
    - Staying informed about new investment tools, financial products, and market trends is vital. It helps investors to not only grasp the current market scenario but also to anticipate future changes.

Engaging with Latest Research and Developments

- **Regular Engagement with New Insights:**
    - Regularly engaging with the latest market research, economic analyses, and investment theories is necessary for making well-informed investment decisions.
- **Staying Informed:**
    - Keeping up-to-date with financial news, academic studies, and industry reports enables investors to understand complex market dynamics and adapt

their strategies accordingly.

Educational Platforms and Continuous Training

- **Leveraging Learning Resources:**
    - Utilizing various educational platforms, such as online courses, financial news websites, and investment analysis tools, provides a foundation for continuous learning.
- **Attending Industry Events:**
    - Participating in seminars, webinars, and industry conferences is an excellent way to stay connected with the latest trends and insights from experts in the field.
- **Networking and Knowledge Exchange:**
    - These events also offer opportunities for networking with other professionals, facilitating the exchange of ideas and experiences.

In conclusion, a commitment to lifelong learning is indispensable for advanced investors. Staying attuned to market evolutions, actively engaging with new research and developments, and continuously seeking educational opportunities are key practices for navigating the complex and ever-changing investment landscape. This ongoing process of learning and adaptation is fundamental to developing robust investment strategies and achieving long-term success.

Adapting Investment Strategies

In the ever-changing world of investing, the capacity to adapt investment strategies in response to new information and evolving market conditions is not just an advantage but a necessity. This section emphasizes the importance of flexibility and responsiveness in investment management, and the need for continuous revision of strategies based on market dynamics.

Flexibility and Responsiveness

- **Proactive Adaptation:**
    - The ability to quickly and effectively adjust investment strategies in response to new market data, economic reports, and global events is crucial. This proactive adaptation helps in seizing emerging market opportunities and protecting the portfolio from unforeseen risks.
- **Capitalizing on Opportunities:**
    - Markets often present fleeting opportunities that require prompt action. Flexible investment strategies enable investors to capitalize on these opportunities, which might be missed by a more rigid approach.
- **Mitigating Risks:**
    - Flexibility also plays a critical role in risk management. By adjusting strategies in response to changing market conditions, investors can better manage potential losses and reduce portfolio volatility.

Revising Strategies Based on Market Dynamics

- **Continuous Strategy Evaluation:**
    - Regular evaluation and revision of investment

strategies are essential to ensure they align with the current market environment. This includes assessing asset allocation, sector exposure, and investment in specific financial instruments.

- **Alignment with Goals and Objectives:**
    - Investment strategies should continually be realigned to fit the investor's evolving goals and risk tolerance. As personal or economic circumstances change, so too should the investment approach.
- **Incorporating New Insights:**
    - Continuous learning and market research provide new insights, which should be integrated into investment strategies. This might involve exploring new sectors, adjusting to economic trends, or responding to technological advancements.

In conclusion, the ability to adapt investment strategies in a timely and effective manner is key for sustained success in investing. Flexibility, responsiveness, and regular strategy revision, aligned with the latest market dynamics and personal investment objectives, are essential practices for navigating the complexities of modern financial markets. This adaptive approach enables investors to stay ahead in a competitive and rapidly evolving investment landscape.

Utilizing Resources and Networks

For advanced investors, effectively utilizing a variety of resources and networks is key to gaining comprehensive market insights and enhancing investment strategies. This section focuses on the importance of leveraging diverse perspectives, building professional networks, and engaging with investment communities.

Leveraging Diverse Perspectives

- **Broadening Knowledge Base:**
    - Accessing a wide array of resources, such as financial news outlets, educational platforms, and sophisticated investment tools, helps investors gain a more rounded understanding of the market.
- **Integrating Varied Insights:**
    - Exposure to diverse perspectives enables investors to view market trends and investment strategies through different lenses, which can lead to more informed decision-making.

Professional Networks and Financial Advisors

- **Building Relationships:**
    - Cultivating a strong professional network within the investment community is invaluable. Relationships with peers, industry experts, and financial advisors can provide a wealth of knowledge and insights.
- **Gaining Expert Advice:**
    - Consulting with financial advisors and market experts can offer in-depth analysis and alternative viewpoints that might not be available through public sources. These professionals can provide

tailored advice, taking into account personal investment goals and risk tolerance.

- **Networking for Opportunities:**
    - A robust network can also be a source of new investment opportunities and collaborations. Engaging with other professionals can open doors to unique investment prospects and partnerships.

Community Engagement and Forums

- **Active Participation in Forums:**
    - Engaging in investment forums and online communities is another effective way to stay informed and connected. These platforms offer a space for sharing and discussing ideas, strategies, and market views with a broader community of investors.
- **Learning from Shared Experiences:**
    - Community discussions can provide practical insights and real-world experiences from diverse investors. Participating in these discussions can reveal common challenges and innovative solutions, benefiting from the collective wisdom of the community.
- **Staying Updated with Trends:**
    - Regular interaction in investment forums helps in keeping up with the latest trends, investor sentiments, and emerging market opportunities.

In conclusion, Chapter 10.3 highlights the significance of utilizing various resources and networks for advanced investors. By leveraging diverse perspectives, building strong professional relationships, and actively participating in investment communities, investors can enhance their knowledge, uncover new opportunities, and refine their investment strategies. This comprehensive approach to resource and network utilization is integral to navigating the multifaceted world of investing successfully.

Appendix A: Glossary of Advanced Investment Terms

In the realm of advanced investing, numerous specialized terms and concepts are essential for a thorough understanding of the field. This appendix provides definitions for key investment terms, offering a valuable resource for both seasoned and aspiring investors.

1. **Alpha**: A measure of an investment's performance relative to a benchmark. It represents the excess return of an investment compared to the return of a benchmark index.
2. **Beta**: A measure of the volatility, or systematic risk, of a security or a portfolio in comparison to the market as a whole.
3. **Efficient Market Hypothesis (EMH)**: A theory that states that it is impossible to "beat the market" because stock market efficiency causes existing share prices to always incorporate and reflect all relevant information.
4. **Modern Portfolio Theory (MPT)**: A theory on how risk-averse investors can construct portfolios to optimize or maximize expected return based on a given level of market risk.
5. **Post-Modern Portfolio Theory (PMPT)**: An extension of MPT that focuses on the downside risk in investment portfolios and prioritizes the preservation of capital.
6. **Derivatives**: Financial instruments whose value is

dependent upon or derived from one or more underlying assets. Common examples include futures, options, and swaps.

7. **Hedge Funds**: Investment funds that employ various strategies to earn active returns for their investors. They are often open to a limited range of investors and can use a wider range of investment techniques than other funds.
8. **Arbitrage**: The simultaneous purchase and sale of an asset to profit from a difference in the price in different markets or formats.
9. **Leverage**: The use of borrowed money (debt) to amplify returns from an investment. While it can increase potential returns, it also increases potential losses.
10. **Short Selling**: The sale of a security that the seller does not own, with the belief that the price will decline, allowing it to be bought back at a lower price.
11. **Liquidity**: The ease with which an asset or security can be converted into cash without affecting its market price.
12. **Diversification**: A risk management strategy that mixes a wide variety of investments within a portfolio to minimize the impact of any single security's performance.
13. **Yield Curve**: A line that plots interest rates, at a set point in time, of bonds having equal credit quality but differing maturity dates. The slope of the yield curve gives an idea of future interest rate changes and economic activity.
14. **Volatility**: A statistical measure of the dispersion of returns for a given security or market index, often measured by the standard deviation or variance between returns.
15. **Risk Parity**: An investment strategy that seeks to allocate risk evenly across various components of a portfolio, rather than allocating based on dollar amounts or expected returns.

This glossary provides a foundational understanding of key concepts in advanced investing, helping readers to better grasp the complexities and strategies discussed throughout the book.

Appendix B: Key Financial Models and Formulas

In advanced investing, financial models and formulas are essential tools for analysis, valuation, and decision-making. This appendix provides an overview of key financial models and formulas widely used in the investment world.

1. **Capital Asset Pricing Model (CAPM)**:
   - **Formula**: Expected Return = Risk-Free Rate + Beta * (Market Return - Risk-Free Rate)
   - **Purpose**: CAPM is used to determine the expected return of an asset, considering its risk in relation to the market.
2. **Discounted Cash Flow (DCF) Model**:
   - **Formula**: NPV = ∑ (CFt / (1 + r)^t), where CFt is the cash flow in period t, and r is the discount rate.
   - **Purpose**: The DCF model calculates the present value of an investment based on its expected future cash flows.
3. **Black-Scholes Model** (for pricing options):
   - **Formula**: C = S0N(d1) - Xe^(-rt)N(d2), where C is the call option price, S0 is the current stock price, X is the strike price, r is the risk-free interest

rate, and t is the time to maturity.
  - **Purpose**: Used to calculate the theoretical value of European put and call options.
4. **Dividend Discount Model (DDM)**:
  - **Formula**: P = D / (k - g), where P is the present value of the stock, D is the dividend per share, k is the required rate of return, and g is the growth rate.
  - **Purpose**: DDM is used to value a stock by using predicted dividends and discounting them back to present value.
5. **Modern Portfolio Theory (MPT) Formulas**:
  - **Efficient Frontier Calculation**: Optimization model to balance risk and return in a portfolio.
  - **Purpose**: Helps in constructing an optimal portfolio offering the maximum possible expected return for a given level of risk.
6. **Sharpe Ratio**:
  - **Formula**: Sharpe Ratio = (Rx - Rf) / StdDev(Rx), where Rx is the return of the investment, Rf is the risk-free rate, and StdDev(Rx) is the standard deviation of the return.
  - **Purpose**: Measures the performance of an investment compared to a risk-free asset, after adjusting for its risk.
7. **Gordon Growth Model** (for stock valuation):
  - **Formula**: P = D1 / (r - g), where P is the price of the stock, D1 is the expected dividend per share one year from now, r is the required rate of return, and g is the growth rate of dividends.

- Purpose: Used to determine the intrinsic value of a stock based on a future series of dividends that grow at a constant rate.

8. **Beta Coefficient**:
    - **Formula**: Beta = Covariance(Return of Asset, Return of Market) / Variance(Return of Market)
    - **Purpose**: Measures the volatility of an asset or portfolio in relation to the overall market.
9. **Internal Rate of Return (IRR)**:
    - **Formula**: The discount rate at which the net present value (NPV) of all the cash flows (both positive and negative) from a project or investment equals zero.
    - **Purpose**: Used to evaluate the attractiveness of a project or investment.
10. **Net Present Value (NPV)**:
    - **Formula**: NPV = ∑ (Rt / (1 + i)^t) - Initial Investment, where Rt is the net cash inflow-outflows during a single period t, i is the discount rate, and t is the number of time periods.
    - **Purpose**: Used to calculate the profitability of a projected investment or project.

These models and formulas are fundamental to financial analysis and investment decision-making. They provide a framework for evaluating risk, return, valuation, and the overall financial viability of investment opportunities.

Appendix C: Resources for Further Learning

For those looking to deepen their understanding of advanced investment concepts and strategies, a multitude of resources are available. This appendix lists various resources across different mediums that can serve as valuable tools for further learning in the field of investing.

Books and Publications

1. **"The Intelligent Investor" by Benjamin Graham**:
    - A foundational book in the world of investing, offering principles and strategies for intelligent investing.
2. **"Security Analysis" by Benjamin Graham and David Dodd**:
    - A comprehensive guide on value investing, providing in-depth analysis techniques for evaluating investments.
3. **Financial Newspapers and Magazines**:
    - Publications like The Wall Street Journal, Financial Times, Bloomberg Businessweek, and The Economist offer insights into current market trends and financial news.

Online Courses and Educational Platforms

1. **Coursera, Udemy, and edX**:
    - These platforms offer courses on various topics in finance and investing, taught by experts from leading universities and institutions.
2. **CFA Institute Resources**:
    - The Chartered Financial Analyst (CFA) Institute offers educational resources and professional development programs in investment management.

Professional Organizations and Networking

1. **CFA Society and Other Investment Groups**:
    - Joining professional organizations like the CFA Society can provide networking opportunities and access to industry events, seminars, and workshops.
2. **LinkedIn Groups**:
    - Participating in investment-focused LinkedIn groups can offer networking opportunities and access to a community of professionals.

Research and Analysis Tools

1. **Bloomberg Terminal, Morningstar, and Yahoo Finance**:
    - These tools provide comprehensive financial data, analytics, and insights for market research and investment analysis.
2. **Financial Modeling Software**:
    - Learning to use financial modeling software can enhance analytical capabilities for investment evaluation.

Podcasts and Webinars

1. **Investment Podcasts**:
   - Podcasts such as "The Investors Podcast" and "Invest Like the Best" offer discussions on market trends and investment strategies.
2. **Webinars and Online Talks**:
   - Many financial institutions and investment firms host webinars and online talks that delve into various aspects of investing.

Regulatory Bodies and Financial News

1. **Securities and Exchange Commission (SEC)**:
   - The SEC's website provides access to regulatory filings and educational resources on investment products and markets.
2. **Financial News Websites**:
   - Staying updated with financial news websites helps in keeping abreast of market developments and regulatory changes.

In conclusion, Appendix C offers a comprehensive list of resources for those interested in furthering their knowledge in advanced investing. From classic books and online courses to professional organizations, research tools, and podcasts, these resources cover a broad spectrum of learning methods and areas of interest. Engaging with these resources can significantly enhance one's understanding and proficiency in the complex and ever-changing world of investment.

Epilogue

As we reach the conclusion of this comprehensive journey through the world of advanced investing, it's clear that the landscape of investment is one of constant evolution and complexity. The chapters of this book have navigated through a myriad of topics, from the intricacies of modern and post-modern portfolio theories to the cutting-edge developments in technology-driven investment opportunities.

Reflection on the Investment Journey

- **Dynamic Nature of Investing:**
  - The investment world is dynamic, shaped by continuous changes in markets, technologies, and global economic landscapes. This book has underscored the importance of staying adaptable, informed, and proactive in this ever-changing environment.
- **Core Principles and Innovations:**
  - While the core principles of risk management, diversification, and valuation remain foundational, we've also explored how innovations in technology and finance are creating new opportunities and challenges for investors.

Looking to the Future

- **Embracing Change and Learning:**
    - The future of investing is likely to be marked by rapid advancements in technology, shifts in global economic power, and evolving regulatory landscapes. Embracing continuous learning and adaptation is crucial for success in this future.
- **Sustainable and Ethical Investing:**
    - As the world increasingly focuses on sustainability and ethics, investors are also expected to continue integrating ESG considerations into their strategies, aligning financial goals with broader social and environmental impacts.

The Role of the Investor

- **Beyond Financial Returns:**
    - The role of the investor extends beyond achieving financial returns. It encompasses understanding and contributing to the broader economic and social environment, leveraging investments to drive positive change.
- **Personal Growth and Responsibility:**
    - The journey through advanced investing is not only a pursuit of financial acumen but also personal growth. It carries a responsibility to make informed decisions that consider both individual goals and the collective well-being.

In conclusion, this book is a testament to the intricate and multifaceted nature of advanced investing. It serves not just as a guide to investment strategies and theories, but also as a reminder of the continuous evolution and learning required in the pursuit of investment excellence. As we look to the future, the principles and insights shared here will undoubtedly remain valuable companions for any investor navigating the complex world of finance.

Don't miss out!

Visit the website below and you can sign up to receive emails whenever Rey Regala publishes a new book. There's no charge and no obligation.

https://books2read.com/r/B-A-HURDB-CBCXC

BOOKS 2 READ

Connecting independent readers to independent writers.

Did you love *Mastery in Markets: Advanced Strategies for Seasoned Investors*? Then you should read *Investment Mastery: Elevating Your Strategy*[1] by Rey Regala!

[2]

Welcome to "Investment Mastery: Elevating Your Strategy," a guide crafted for the intermediate investor who seeks to deepen their understanding and enhance their skills in the complex world of investing. This book is born out of a recognition that the journey of an investor is continuous and evolving, demanding ever-greater knowledge and sophistication.

As an intermediate investor, you are no stranger to the basics of investing. You understand the fundamentals of stocks, bonds, mutual funds, and perhaps have dabbled in more advanced areas such as ETFs or real estate. However, the path from being a

1. https://books2read.com/u/3nqD96

2. https://books2read.com/u/3nqD96

knowledgeable beginner to becoming a proficient investor is nuanced and requires a deeper dive into both theory and practice.

This book is structured to build upon your existing foundation, introducing more sophisticated concepts and strategies that are often reserved for professional investors. We delve into advanced portfolio management, explore international markets, dissect alternative investments, and even venture into the psychological aspects of investing. Each chapter not only presents comprehensive insights but also practical examples and case studies, making the concepts relatable and applicable.

Our goal is to empower you to make more informed, strategic decisions. Whether it's understanding the intricacies of market cycles, navigating the complexities of tax strategies, or integrating sustainable investing principles into your portfolio, this book is designed to be your companion in this journey.

We also recognize that investing is not just about strategies and returns; it's deeply personal and intertwined with your life goals and values. Hence, we emphasize creating a lifelong investment plan that resonates with your personal aspirations and adapts to life's various stages.

Also by Rey Regala

Investing

First Steps in Investing: A Beginner's Guide
Investment Mastery: Elevating Your Strategy
Mastery in Markets: Advanced Strategies for Seasoned Investors

www.ingramcontent.com/pod-product-compliance
Lightning Source LLC
LaVergne TN
LVHW050300210926
848481LV00014BA/242
* 9 7 9 8 2 2 3 1 1 4 2 8 4 *